University Science and Engineering
Libraries

CONTRIBUTIONS IN
LIBRARIANSHIP AND
INFORMATION SCIENCE

Series Editor: *Paul Wasserman*

Frontiers in Librarianship: Proceedings of the Change Institute, 1969
School of Library and Information Services, University of Maryland

Subject Retrieval in the Seventies: New Directions. An International
Symposium
Hans (Hanan) Wellisch and *Thomas D. Wilson*, Editors

Quantitative Methods in Librarianship: Standards, Research, Management
Irene Braden Hoadley and *Alice S. Clark*, Editors

Public Relations for Libraries: Essays in Communications Techniques
Allan Angoff, Editor

Human Memory and Knowledge: A Systems Approach
Glynn Harmon

Libraries in the Political Scene: Georg Leyh and German Librarianship,
1933-1953
Marta L. Dosa

Information Retrieval and Documentation in Chemistry
Charles H. Davis and *James E. Rush*

Illustrative Computer Programming for Libraries: Selected Examples for
Information Specialists
Charles H. Davis

University Science and Engineering Libraries

Their Operation, Collections, and Facilities

ELLIS MOUNT

Contributions in Librarianship and Information Science
Number 15

GREENWOOD PRESS

Westport, Connecticut • London, England

Library of Congress Cataloging in Publication Data

Mount, Ellis.
University science and engineering libraries, their
operation, collections, and facilities.

(Contributions in librarianship and information
science ; no. 15)
Includes bibliographical references and index.
1. Libraries, University and college.   2. Scientific
libraries.   3. Engineering libraries.   I. Title.
II. Series.
Z675.U5M68   026'.5   74-34562
ISBN 0-8371-7955-6

Library of Congress Catalog Card Number: 74-34562
ISBN: 0-8371-7955-6

First published in 1975

Greenwood Press, a division of Williamhouse-Regency Inc.
51 Riverside Avenue, Westport, Connecticut 06880

Printed in the United States of America

Contents

Illustrations

Preface

Library service at universities for the disciplines of engineering and the sciences is an important part of the overall library activities at such institutions. Despite this importance the literature on this subject is not extensive, the bulk of it located in scattered periodical articles. It is hoped that this book will help fill the literary gap that exists.

This work covers a wide selection of topics in order to discuss all the major aspects of the science-engineering library service. It should probably be most useful to professional librarians who are new to this area of librarianship, including not only those just entering the profession but also experienced librarians who have not been exposed to science and engineering at universities. Hopefully, the book will also provide food for thought for some librarians already working in such libraries, as well as give library school students a preview of what to expect there.

The plan of the book is to proceed from broad topics, such as the general nature of the libraries involved and their organization, to more specific points, e.g., staffing, collection development, reference services, uses of computers, and the planning of library facilities. The characteristics of the many types of literature and nonprint materials required in such libraries will also be described. Samples, selected from the vast number of available items, will illustrate each type of material.

In many instances library services in these subjects are similar at colleges and universities; hence, to some extent the book may be applicable to libraries at colleges as well as at universities. Comparisons are also made with special libraries and technical library divisions in public libraries.

Appreciation is hereby expressed for the valuable assistance given by many of my colleagues.

University Science and Engineering Libraries

1

The Nature of Technical Libraries
at Universities

There are several types of libraries that specialize in science and engineering: those at universities; special departments in large public libraries; and special libraries, not generally available to the public, that specialize in a particular aspect of science or technology.

A discussion of the nature of science-engineering libraries at universities should include a comparison of them with the technically-oriented libraries in public and private organizations. Still another useful way to describe them is to discuss the ways in which they differ from other types of libraries at universities, such as journalism or music libraries. There are marked differences between technical and nontechnical libraries on any campus, such as kinds of services offered, emphasis of collections, access after closing hours, etc.

In many respects it is impossible to describe the "average" university library devoted to technical subjects. Such a library varies substantially from one university to another, and even from one side of a campus to the other (although in some of their characteristics they are remarkably similar). Therefore, in describing particular features of these libraries, the variations that exist will also be emphasized.

General Nature

Size of Collections and Facilities—Probably no characteristic of scientific-technical libraries at universities differs as much from one technical library to another as the size—both of their collections and their physical facilities. At one end of the spectrum can be found libraries with less than ten thousand volumes and occupying only one or two thousand square feet, while at the other end might be facilities with several floors, totaling tens of thousands of square feet, with collections well over a quarter of a million. Probably the main reason for the great variations is the type of organization chosen, whether centralization or decentralization is practiced. A survey of twenty-two universities demonstrates the effect of organizational patterns on the size and operating conditions of their technical libraries.[1] They are closely related topics. Other aspects of such libraries, including reference service and staffing characteristics, are also given in that survey.

Aside from centralized science-engineering systems at universities, the larger campus library units dealing with these subjects tend to be found at the schools and institutes devoted solely to science and engineering, where there is normally only one library. This library is essentially devoted to these disciplines, and is the equivalent of the main library found at most universities. For example, at Georgia Institute of Technology there is only the one central library, plus one small departmental library. The bulk of their collection (over three-quarters of a million volumes) is centered on science and engineering. Thus the main library at that institution is concentrated on technical literature, with less attention given to the collections in related fields, such as accounting, management, and the humanities, needed for carrying out well-rounded programs of instruction. On the campuses of universities, however, the main library usually has a collection in the humanities and/or social sciences, so that the largest collections in one library unit on such campuses are not located in the engineering and science libraries.

As mentioned previously, sci-tech facilities range from tiny, crowded areas, usually poorly furnished and unattractive, to handsome, spacious, centralized libraries, sometimes having three or four floors, with the most modern of equipment and furnishings. Frequently, the same university has a rather motley assortment of outdated and modern facilities for the sciences and engineering. The more units there are, the more likely the facilities are disparate. This is not to say, however, that centralization per se is the permanent answer to having modern facilities, since a single unit devoted to technical materials can become crowded and old-fashioned just as easily as several small units can. One does not have to look hard to find instances of technically oriented institutions with one library which is old and unsatisfactory. By contrast, some institutions, of which Stanford University could be considered as an example, manage to maintain relatively high quality physical facilities for technical libraries in spite of having over a dozen such units.

Staffing—The organizational plan in use is also the primary factor governing the staff sizes in science-engineering libraries. Those universities with decentralized units usually have several libraries with one professional staff member assigned to each, while other universities use one librarian to supervise two or three units. In contrast, centralized units may have half a dozen or more professional librarians on hand to provide reference services and supervision. Catalogers are rarely assigned to sci-tech libraries because central cataloging departments at most universities are usually located in the main library, not in a science library— even a centralized science library. One sci-tech library which has a larger than usual staff and collection is the science library at the University of Georgia. This library is housed in a separate three-story building, has a collection of over a quarter of a million volumes, and employs a professional staff of six.

Librarians in decentralized university sci-tech libraries often tend to feel like jacks-of-all-trades because they combine supervision with reference work, collection development (including selection of materials), liaison with the central cataloging unit, and a multitude of other duties. On the other hand, centralization tends to create more specialized positions for librarians, such as doing only reference work or collection development.

The sci-tech units, whether centralized or decentralized, are usually supervised by an experienced librarian with a strong science background. While a few successful librarians in such positions have managed to do well in spite of a nonscientific background, in general lack of background is a handicap.

Collections—The sizes of collections might range from five thousand volumes to five hundred thousand, depending upon the degree of centralization, the scope of the subjects included in each library, and other factors. The total volumes devoted to sci-tech subjects in universities often total well over half a million. At institutions devoted almost entirely to technical subjects it is not uncommon to have total collections of more than one million volumes.

The most important type of literature in science and engineering libraries is by far the periodical, together with other serials, such as annuals. Periodicals are more useful than books simply because they are far more current and their articles are more specific than books. However, collections in such libraries could not exist without textbooks, handbooks, tables, and a multitude of other monographic works. Another major element in many sci-tech libraries is the technical report collection, most of which is sponsored by or prepared by government agencies. In some areas of science, such as geology, libraries rely heavily on their own collections of maps.

Although numerically the predominant literature format of most libraries is still the full-size volume, the growing collections of microforms and audiovisual materials indicate that traditional book formats are being increasingly challenged by relatively newer modes of information.

Reader Services—The most commonly used aspect of reader services is, of course, the circulation of materials. Hardly a student exists who has not had to use reserve books for required reading in his courses, even if his experience with libraries is minimal. In preparing papers students often realize their limited experience in finding technical information; the wiser ones will therefore ask for help in finding their way around. The reference librarians' assistance is often centered on acquainting students with likely reference tools to use, or ways of finding pertinent subject headings in the card catalog. They cannot go so far as to locate and recommend specific detailed citations for a student to use, for the librarian must not get in the position of doing the student's work.

With graduate students and faculty members, reference work can be more precise and, consequently, more demanding. Occasional bibliographies are requested by faculty members who have learned to rely on their libraries for such help. However, most university faculty members do not make as much reference use of their libraries as the staffs involved would prefer. Word of mouth is often the best advertisement, which takes some time to establish in most university settings.

Growing attention is being given to library instructional services—the various means for teaching students, faculty members, and research workers the proper use of technical literature. Activities range from library tours to full-credit courses, from audiovisual presentations to brief lectures in a professor's class on literature related to that subject. Another area of growing importance is that of utilizing computer-stored data bases for retrieving information. Tapes for data bases may be available on the campus, particularly on larger ones, or the libraries may be able to reach data centers located far from the campus through suitable telephone lines. The latter practice has the advantage of offering a greater selection of data bases without the expense of handling tapes locally. Long-term contracts for such service are common. Also popular now is another system—that of one-time, single-charge queries which can be ended whenever the user of the terminal desires, with charges based almost solely on elapsed time. In most cases the user relies on the data center to mail complete citations and abstracts, if any, rather than take up time at the terminal.

Another professional activity which could be called a reader service is collection development. While not always so classified, it is done for the ultimate benefit of the reader and thus might be termed a reader service. It includes selection of materials, whether gifts or purchases, weeding of collections, and decisions about the many other factors involved in building suitable collections. Such work is severely handicapped by lack of subject expertise and bibliographic judgment. A library full of second-rate selections from publishers who turn out inferior works is a far cry from the well-selected collection of major works from the top publishers.

Many librarians have found a happy medium between complete reliance on and studied indifference to faculty recommendations for the collection. Either extreme is unsuitable, the one because some professors have a bias toward certain subjects or works, and the other because it implies that libraries are organized without regard for the need of their chief users. Locally prepared statements of what should be collected, developed with the aid of users, are invaluable documents. These guide librarians in making selections in the absence of user requests and in evaluating requests that have been received.

Comparison with Other Types of Libraries

The remainder of this chapter will be devoted to comparing scientific and engineering libraries to other types of libraries, both university and nonuniversity. It will be seen that there are many similarities, yet each type is distinct and different.

Other University and College Libraries—Most university library systems consist of the main library and a collection of smaller libraries, of which the technical libraries constitute but one segment. The record for number of distinct units is probably held by Harvard University, which has approximately one hundred units. By contrast there is Johns Hopkins University with one main library and only one other unit. Obviously wide variations exist on different campuses. Local preference, tradition, and existence of usable facilities rather than pure logic, often determine the number and type of library units.

As previously mentioned, most main libraries at universities with many units are devoted to the humanities or social sciences, and perhaps have all-purpose undergraduate libraries or reserve rooms as added features.

There are many nontechnical libraries at most universities devoted to such subjects as music, sociology, journalism, or any of a score of other specific disciplines; they are as varied in size, organizational patterns, and services rendered as the science-engineering libraries are. Although overall descriptions are difficult to make, some differences between the technical and nontechnical libraries can be pointed out.

One obvious difference is in their collections. Periodicals are not nearly as significant to some subjects as they are to science and engineering. This is not to say that they are unimportant in the humanities or social sciences, but books probably still outshine journals in those disciplines. Even more a specialty of sci-tech libraries are technical reports, patents, and specifications for commercial products, which are of practically no interest in other disciplines.

Until the appearance of census data on readily available computer tapes, most nonscience libraries had little contact with machine-readable data bases on a national or international scale; in contrast these were well known to engineering and science libraries. Most computer activity in the humanities and social sciences is in the form of individual research projects, often little-known outside a small circle of specialists. There are, in addition, the many readily available tape services, mentioned previously, which cover significant collections of data, unknown to the humanities and social sciences until the Bureau of the Census created computer-tape records for the latest census data. It is unlikely that computer-based data bases will ever have the significance outside technical areas that they have within, but at least nontechnical applications are more feasible now than formerly.

Finding librarians with suitable subject backgrounds is generally considered more difficult for science and engineering libraries than for their nontechnical counterparts. The primary reason is that fewer library school students are trained in or interested in such positions. So university technical libraries are sometimes manned by librarians with little or no training in the subjects covered. Recent overall reductions in the number of positions available have ameliorated this situation somewhat, but over the years such positions are usually difficult to fill properly. Competition with industry for those with good technical backgrounds is often a problem.

College libraries can rarely afford the luxury of separate libraries for different disciplines, much less special librarians trained in the disciplines involved. So the selection and use of scientific materials at colleges is often just another duty for general librarians working in all disciplines.

Few colleges have engineering courses, thus technical collections at such schools are more apt to concentrate on the so-called pure sciences—mathematics, chemistry, physics, perhaps some earth science—with little or no coverage of engineering except as it might relate to these courses. This is usually on a minor scale.

Public Libraries—Like university science and engineering libraries, the large public libraries, such as the research units of the New York Public Library, have very strong collections and well-trained staffs. On the other hand, the small or average-sized public library has little in common with university units. The average small public library has neither the funds nor the reader interest to warrant building up highly technical research collections, and, of course, special staff members for technical subject areas would be out of the question.

Thus a comparison of university science and engineering libraries with public libraries is meaningful only when we consider those public libraries large enough to have departments for science and engineering. There are some very outstanding examples of public libraries with such an arrangement, having good collections. Only a few have the funds, however, to build up collections to rival those of university libraries, or to hire librarians with strong subject backgrounds in these disciplines. Going to the extreme of the research units of New York Public Library, whose collections surpass those of many universities and where the staff is well grounded in the subjects, the situation is closer to university standards for collections and personnel than to public libraries.

The more transient patronage of public libraries does, of course, distinguish them from campus units on that score.

One notable library, which was once open to the public and specialized in science, technology, and medicine, is the John Crerar Library in Chicago, which has a fine, large collection in these subjects. It is now serving as the library for the Illinois Institute of Technology in that city.

The largest science departments in the largest public libraries are usually looking for about the same kind of librarians as university technical libraries are, and the salary levels are roughly comparable. Stability of positions and vacation allowances are also very similar in the two types of libraries. Tuition allowances for university employees constitute one difference, however.

Special Libraries—This group of libraries primarily serves a specific clientele with a rather narrow range of interests. In a broad sense science and engineering libraries at universities or in large public libraries belong to this category, but they tend to be larger than the average special library and to serve a larger group of users.

The average special library has one or two professional librarians, plus supporting staff members (the term for nonprofessional employees). It serves the employees of a particular company or agency, such as a corporation, bank, laboratory, company of auditors, art museum, or government bureau. Their clientele, like the university faculty, is more stable compared to that of public libraries and students at universities.

Collections in special libraries tend to be much more specialized than those in typical university libraries. Both types may have the same basic important journals and texts, but the special library often collects in depth on some limited aspect of a more basic discipline. For example, a library for a steel company would have not only all the major English and foreign journals for general metallurgy and metal working, but it would also have minor journals touching on some aspect of steel and its applications. In addition to texts on the subject, it would seek out pamphlets, patents, conference reports—literally anything of a serious nature pertaining to this metal.

Unlike the university library, the special library has the funds and space to devote itself intently to each topic in its collection. However, it has a rather limited number of topics in which to specialize.

Reference service in special libraries tends to be more intense than that in university units, primarily because their relatively stable patrons enable close relationships to develop. Another factor is that the special library is geared primarily to the specialized needs of the employees, whereas a university sci-tech library serves a more general purpose— support of a relatively broad educational program for graduates and undergraduates. Twenty professors in a department at a university may have twenty completely different research aims, much broader than one might find in a commercial research laboratory. Hence, the faculty and research employees at a university do not expect the same depth of collections and awareness of their projects that they might find in a typical special library.

In regard to staffing, special libraries often attract librarians away from universities because of their generally higher pay. This is often more true for librarians with science or engineering backgrounds than for those with liberal arts or nontechnical training. Although the latter find employment in special libraries, the better paying library positions in industry often require technical backgrounds. On the other hand, vacations and fringe benefits in industry and commerce rarely equal those at universities. In addition, university librarians and their spouses or children often have free tuition for certain courses, which is equivalent to a large sum of money in these days of rising tuition costs.

Clerical help, especially that of part-time students, is frequently more abundant in universities, where many supporting staff members are enrolled in courses on a free tuition plan, thus providing a high level of employee ability not always found in the clerical workers of industry. Obviously, no absolute statements on this subject can stand close examination, as there are many devoted, bright, nonprofessional employees outside academic circles. It may be said, however, that the average person on that level at universities is better educated than his or her counterpart in industry. This, plus the fine part-time help provided by students, gives most university librarians a strong labor source.

Positions in university libraries are more stable and more resistant to the ups and downs of the economy than are those in some special libraries in industry and commerce, where the marketplace has a greater effect on employment levels. The campuses may have more lower-paid positions, but as universities cannot exist without libraries, the jobs there are more secure. Unfortunately, many executives in industry and commerce tend to think of their libraries as expendable, particularly when funding problems arise. This sort of thinking is only slowly evaporating as more and more special librarians are proving to their employers the real worth of an information service.

One of the best descriptions of special libraries is found in the book by Strauss,[2] which concentrates on libraries devoted to science and engineering, and describes their organization, budgets, collections, and services. In addition, it lists many examples of each type of technical literature of interest in technical libraries. In one of its tables it shows that the average special library has a total staff size of around five persons, while the number of engineers and scientists served per staff member ranges from 30 to 122, the latter being the most recent figure.[3] The work also cites Special Libraries Association figures which show that of thirty-eight hundred special libraries almost one thousand had one to two staff members.[4] Thus, such libraries tend to be small and highly specialized in their collections and scope.

Notes

[1]Ellis Mount, *University Science and Engineering Libraries— A Survey*, 1972, 26 p. (Available from ERIC Document Reproduction Service, Bethesda, Md. 20014, as ED 068 108.)

[2]Lucille J. Strauss, and others. *Scientific and Technical Libraries: Their Organization and Administration*, 2d ed. (New York: Wiley, 1972), 450 p.

[3]Ibid., p. 38.

[4]Ibid., p. 39.

2

Organizational Patterns and Locations of Libraries

Libraries at universities are characteristically organized in a great variety of ways within the overall library systems. Moreover, these systems operate many different physical units. The effects of organization and location of units on library service, size, efficiency, and staffing are far-reaching.

General Organizational Patterns

When universities were first developed in the United States, the library was a very simple operation, housed in one modest-sized building. As libraries grew, larger and larger buildings were required. Often the campus expanded in size at the same time. Finally, pressure among library users led a university to create a subunit of the main library, perhaps at the insistence of a particular department of instruction. One subunit led to two, and before long the process of decentralizing university libraries was under way. Some universities developed scores of departmental libraries. In comparison to Harvard's total of over ninety units, a system with around thirty units, as is the case at Columbia

13

University, looks relatively centralized. Yet today some really large universities have only a handful of library units because they have decided to stand firm on the subject of consolidation. The large campus of the University of Georgia at Athens is a case in point. Besides the main library the entire campus is served by a law library and a science library, although there are small department-run, key book collections for quick reference use.

The proponents of each system contend that their methods are best. Certainly each system does have its advantages, although the tide seems to be turning toward certain methods of consolidation. Different ways of administering these libraries often depend upon the number and location of the physical units. Various administrative plans now in vogue, including the aspect of the physical locations commonly found in each plan, will now be discussed.

In general, the organizational patterns can be put into three categories: centralization, decentralization, or miscellaneous systems (somewhere in between the two extremes). These categories have been given considerable attention in the literature. Marianne Cooper's paper, for example, gives a very good account of the types of arrangements used for science libraries, and also cites many of the better known articles on the subject.[1] After discussing the pros and cons of each type, she concludes with the observation: "The organizational patterns of science and technology libraries result from compromises between the needs of users, as they see them, and the practical requirements of budgets and administrative control, as seen by the librarians." This often seems to be the case, although ideally administrative decisions about library locations should be based as much on the desire for better service to users as on the practical needs of budgets and administrative concerns. The problem seems to be that of convincing users that better service will result from a given administrative-designed plan of library organization and location. Many discussions with users may be needed to clarify the library's reasoning, but such time-consuming negotiations are necessary if librarians and users are to avoid getting into adversary-type situations, with resulting hard feelings. If library administrators cannot offer better service, but have only budgetary considerations to present, they should not be surprised if their plans are not immediately accepted by dubious faculty members and students. The university's clientele has a right to expect the concept of improved service to be included in all such discussions and decisions.

Decentralized Library Units

In this chapter it is assumed that all the library units at a university are part of an overall library system, reporting eventually to the same director of libraries and sharing the same overall budget. However, this is not always the case, for at some universities different departments of instruction maintain their own libraries, hire their own librarians, and provide their own budgets. Harvard is an eminent example. Of the ninety or so units making up the library complex there, not all of them belong to the geneal library system; several in fact are maintained by separate departments. Such a situation makes for difficulties in cooperative activities, uniform procedures and standards, and coordination of collections. No doubt it has very strong proponents among the instructional departments served by their own libraries, but the current trend is definitely toward a single library system for a given university. Of all the different types of libraries at a university, law and medical libraries are the most likely to be operated by the schools they serve, if any are in this category. But this arrangement is by no means found at most universities, since the majority of them operate all official library units, no matter what their subject matter.

Systems of decentralized libraries can be further subdivided into different classes, but we will not give an exhaustive account of all possible arrangements here. Perhaps it will suffice to say that no two universities are alike as regards the number and organization of their library units. Thus decentralization can—and usually does—take various forms. It can range from complete decentralization, with each subject having its own library, to some consolidation in certain subjects. For example, there is now a trend toward combining libraries for health sciences and biology into one life sciences library, while at the same time maintaining separate libraries for engineering, mathematics, chemistry, and the like. The geography of campus building locations is often an important factor in such decisions.

Probably the most attractive feature of decentralization to the users is convenience of location; with decentralization the libraries are usually in the same building or in a closely knit cluster of buildings, serving a particular discipline. Another feature which users appreciate is the staff's acquaintance with the regular users and their particular interests. This creates a homey, informal atmosphere which many users prefer to the more impersonal ambience of some centralized units.

On the negative side, users of decentralized units are now fully aware of the limitations on building the collections, particularly in recent years, as shrinking budgets and rising costs of literature have placed severe restrictions on the number of books and serials that can be purchased. Overlapping of periodical subscriptions between small library units, once done with little concern for costs, is more and more being eliminated because budgets can no longer allow it. As for hours of service, few if any decentralized systems can offer professional library service in the evenings or on weekends. As a consequence, users must contact the librarians during the day on weekdays or forego professional reference assistance altogether. Even the weekday schedules are less than what users feel is a minimum.

As for the librarians and their staffs, the staffing is usually rather thin, with the librarian having to tend to such a multitude of tasks that there is little time for developing special services. The inevitable staff shortages that occur because of absences or vacations are most critical in units with only a few regular staff members. In such cases loaning from one unit to another is the only solution. Such an arrangement is not very satisfactory if each unit has developed routines and systexs different from those in related libraries. Adjustment to different libraries is harder in such cases.

Restricting decentralized libraries to one subject area means that if a librarian trained in that particular subject can be found, then the match of staff and subject served is beneficial. However, competition for technically trained librarians makes this a difficult problem for administrators. Further complicating this picture is the relatively small number of job-seekers at one time who have the exact subject background desired for a particular university sci-tech library.

The growing importance of certain services involving audiovisual aids, computer terminals, or microforms presents a financial burden in any library system. Furnishing units with the expensive equipment required and trying to duplicate the equipment at numerous small science-/engineering units are often beyond the ability of the average university. As a result, sharing of equipment or centralization of it in one unit is the only alternative.

Although it is theoretically possible for all individual small library units to report to one person in the library administration, this is rarely the case. To expect one administrator to be able to handle twenty or thirty different libraries, in library systems of that size, would create a difficult supervisory and administrative problem. Perhaps in view of this situation different administrative patterns have been developed, the most common of which is that of grouping library units at a university into divisions. There may be separate divisions for the arts, the social sciences, and the sciences, including engineering.

The latter arrangement has been in common use for many years. The number of library units per division will vary greatly, but probably ranges from five to ten. At Columbia University, where such a plan was adopted in 1964 for the science division; eight units were set up covering the subjects of biology, chemistry, engineering, geology, mathematics, physics/astronomy, and psychology, all on the main campus. In addition, off campus there was a distant unit covering related earth sciences, such as oceanography. The mathematics library unit also included what is known as the science library, in which general science, history of science, and scientific biographies are found.

Some large library systems have broken the sciences and engineering into two groups. For example, the University of California at Los Angeles has four libraries which make up a divisional grouping consisting just of the physical sciences and engineering, while the other main grouping is made up of the biomedical units.

Much depends, of course, upon the location of classroom and office buildings for the various departments, the overall size of the campus, and the degree of authority which departments assume in such matters. If a university administration lets departments of instruction decide on the number and location of library units, in general, no department will be clamoring for elimination of their separate units in favor of consolidated ones. Faculties may agree to consolidation but they rarely initiate such action. As each local campus situation differs, it is not possible to prescribe what any one school should do. There are certainly basic guidelines, but an exact formula is not feasible for deciding such matters.

Much of the effectiveness of a system has to do with other factors, such as the quality of the staff, the amount of money available, or the level of service acceptable to a given set of faculty members. With a large budget and an excellent staff, almost any system will work, but most universities do not have such a luxury now. More and more care is being taken to get the most service out of every dollar spent. For these reasons consolidation is finding more and more favor. The desire to give better service at a lower overall cost, or at least at a cost lower than a similar service would cost if given with highly decentralized units, is a strong motivation now.

A good discussion of the pros and cons of this matter is found in an article by Waldhart and Zweifel.[2] They urge that scientific planning techniques—rather than political influence, or ignorance of the possibilities of finding improved service through changes—be utilized to a greater extent in deciding on library plans. A librarian unacquainted with the workings of faculties and other campus forces may want to read the article by Straus.[3] Other readings giving more details about departmental libraries are worth pursuing.[4]

Consolidated Library Units

It is obvious from the preceding section that serious faults have been found in decentralized library systems. They include higher total costs for all units per hour of being open (particularly in the evenings and weekends); difficulties of providing professional reference service at all hours; overlapping of collections; lack of proper quantities of expensive equipment; and limitations on what the professional staff can do to provide more sophisticated reference and instructional services.

While no organizational plan can solve all the problems of university libraries, it does appear that as far as the librarians are concerned a certain degree of consolidation offers many advantages. For example, consolidation lowers staffing and maintenance costs (a group of individual small units would be more costly) and enables better utilization of staff members. Furthermore, it gives professionals a chance to specialize in some aspect of library work, such as reference or instructional service, and it makes equipping of one unit with expensive audiovisual, microform, and computer equipment much more feasible.

What needs to be made clear to the users, in most cases, is that better service also accompanies such a consolidation. Many patrons are so accustomed to a small library in their building that they find it hard to think of any advantage of going to a larger unit outside their building. Thus, the library staff has a selling job on its hands if it is to convince users of the merits of consolidation.

A larger collection in which to browse or find required readings, longer hours, more professional help, and probably more comfortable and more attractive quarters are sufficient to convince many users of the worth of walking to such a unit. Others need more powerful arguments. The funding problems created by today's economy should give anyone on a campus the additional impetus to accept a better system. Duplication of serials and monographs, except for the most important items, is becoming virtually impossible in most universities. It literally means that for every title duplicated there will be one less unique title in the collection.

As in the case of decentralization, each campus is a case unto itself as to the type and degree of consolidation needed. Similar to the example of the University of Georgia is Johns Hopkins University in Baltimore, where virtually complete consolidation took place. At one time Hopkins, despite its rather small campus, had seven different libraries serving sixteen departments of science and technology. Nathalie Nicholson surveyed the situation and saw three possible paths: to leave the situation unchanged, to create a new library just for science/technology, or to consolidate all units.[5] She recommended complete consolidation, the plan which was eventually adopted. Now a new consolidated library has replaced the small units, although one additional unit is still operating outside the main library. For a campus its size, there was little or no justification for continuation of decentralized units.

A recent survey of various consolidation plans at universities showed that very often the price for faculty acceptance of a consolidated science library was the additional creation of small departmental reading rooms.[6] The typical room was restricted more or less to faculty members and graduate students. It had ten or so runs of key journals selected by the faculty, often with their own donated copies forming the nucleus for such an arrangement, with certain reference books and key monographs, and perhaps one periodical index covering ten years or more. Thus they now were able to answer many of their inquiries in their own building and to browse through the most important periodicals. This arrangement cut down on the number of trips they had to make to the science library and, in general, this collection seemed to be heavily used. Sometimes a departmental secretary was responsible for watching over the collection, but in other universities a member of the library supporting staff and/or part-time student on the library payroll helped to keep things in order and monitor the circulation. At the University of British Columbia the library went further and actually trained departmental personnel in the rudiments of taking care of the collection and in using simple reference tools. It also contributed money for the building of the collection. Usually one such reading room per building was sufficient. Such reading rooms are also in existence at Georgia and Johns Hopkins and seem to help smooth the way for general acceptance of the consolidated library. It is, of course, impossible to please all faculty members with such a combination of facilities, but it also would be impossible to please all of them with any kind of facility. The acceptance of the majority of users is usually about the best librarians can hope for.

Another feature of campuses where there were successful consolidated science facilities was the giving of free delivery service to faculty members. This proved to be very much appreciated by the professors. Return of literature was also possible under most such systems. Another factor which helped make centralization acceptable was good photocopy service at the science library, including the taking of orders over the phone and the charging of copies to the faculty members' projects and grants.

In order to make a centralized library more appealing to users from different disciplines, some of them had their browsing section divided into different disciplines, such as one corner for all the new journal issues and books for chemistry, and another corner for physics. The users' needs were thereby catered to. A sympathetic staff who makes an effort to get to know regular patrons and their interests can also do much to make them all feel as much at home as they did in smaller units. If the small units being replaced are crowded, with poor equipment and furnishings, an attractive new centralized library will have several points to its advantage.

For additional material on the question of consolidation, the reader is referred to the writings by Marron,[7] Wells,[8] and Legg.[9] It is a question that university librarians will no doubt continue to face in the foreseeable future. No doubt, too, the trend is toward consolidation for a variety of reasons, of which better service and more efficient operating conditions are the prime ones.

Miscellaneous Examples

In some cases, the type of organization and unit location vary from that described in the previous sections. One case is that in which the main library of an institution is almost entirely devoted to science and engineering. A prime example is the library at Georgia Institute of Technology, where one main library serves the entire campus, with the exception of one branch library under professional supervision. For a large campus with around eight thousand students this is a case of successful operation of a consolidated unit in circumstances that might not be considered ideal for success. There are three reading rooms under control of departments of instruction, but considering the size of the campus this is a surprisingly low number. As previously mentioned, there are related topics besides technical ones in the main library; the predominant thrust of the collection, however, is toward science and engineering.

Another system is one in which the science-engineering library has its own floor(s) in the main library, so that it is consolidated yet remains a separate entity to the users. Examples may be found at Florida Atlantic University and at Oregon State University. For universities with somewhat smaller collections this seems a very workable plan. The two schools in question had total collections in 1972 of 475,000 and 670,000 volumes, respectively, so that the sci-tech portions could be fitted into one floor of a good-sized library without undue difficulties.

It should be pointed out that at many universities special departments or research institutes are located far from the main campus, so that it is imperative to have a relatively small library at such an installation. The degree of integration of such units with the rest of the library system varies tremendously, depending upon such factors as the degree of difficulty of getting to the main campus, the relation of the institute or department to the rest of the university, and the desire and effort of the library administrators to bring the unit close to the library system. Having a university bus to simplify travel, as well as distributing accession lists, newsletters, and other information from the main campus, are also factors in achieving close relationships.

In conclusion, each university must decide for itself just how much consolidation is feasible, bearing many factors in mind. Consolidation offers many benefits, but library systems will be well advised to discuss plans for centralization carefully with users, acceding to departmental requests for their own small supplementary reading rooms where desired.

Notes

[1]Marianne Cooper, "Organizational Patterns of Academic Science Libraries," *College and Research Libraries* 29, no. 5 (September 1968): 357-363.

[2]Thomas J. Waldhart and Leroy G. Zweifel, "Organizational Patterns of Scientific and Technical Libraries: An Examination of Three Issues," *College and Research Libraries* 34, no. 6 (November 1973): 426-435.

[3]Robert Straus, "Departments and Disciplines: Stasis and Change," *Science* 182, no. 4115 (November 30, 1973): 895-898.

[4]Lawrence Thompson, "The Historical Background of Departmental Collegiate Libraries," *Library Quarterly* 12, no. 1 (January 1942): 49-74. Robert R. Walsh, "Branch Library Planning in Universities," *Library Trends* 18, no. 2 (October 1969): 210-222.

[5]N. W. Nicholson, "Centralization of Science Libraries at Johns Hopkins University." In *Studies in Library Administration Problems* (New Brunswick, N.J.: Rutgers University Press, 1960), 210 p.

[6]Ellis Mount, *University Science and Engineering Libraries—A Survey*, 1972, 26 p. (Available from ERIC Document Reproduction Service, Bethesda, Md. 20014, as ED 068 108.)

[7]Harvey Marron, "Science Libraries: Consolidated/Departmental," *Physics Today* 16, no. 7 (July 1963): 34-36, 38-39.

[8]D. A. Wells, "Individual Departmental Libraries vs. Consolidated Science Libraries," *Physics Today* 14, no. 5 (May 1961): 40-41.

[9]Jean Legg, "Death of the Departmental Library," *Library Resources and Technical Services* 9, no. 3 (Summer 1965): 351-355.

3

Library Administration

Basic Principles

The administration of a separate science or engineering library, or a group or division of them, may vary in emphasis or detail from the administration of a fine arts library or a general university library. However, all these positions rely upon the same basic principles of administration which have a broad application to organizations throughout our society. There have been many books written on administration in general and several on library administration in particular. Therefore, it would be redundant to present a voluminous amount of material on basic principles in this book. Perhaps all that is necessary is to summarize the highlights of selected writings on library administration and to cite those deemed most useful, and then take up specific aspects of administration as they apply to the management of science-engineering libraries on campuses. However, a discussion of most personnel matters will be deferred to the next chapter.

Librarians desiring texts on the operation, administration, and organization of university libraries have several works from which to choose. One of the better known is the text on university libraries by Louis Wilson and Maurice Tauber,[1] which is out of date but remains a useful, detailed study of all aspects of such libraries. It is very well documented and illustrated with charts and tables, and contains copious references to related literature.

The close relationship of college to university libraries is clear from an examination of Guy Lyle's book on the administration of college libraries.[2] Most of his text would provide useful background information for any librarian seeking a career in university libraries, particularly because of its philosophical outlook and the general principles it sets forth.

For a more recent general text, the reader should consult the work by Rogers and Weber.[3] It gives a detailed account of all aspects of university libraries, ranging from financial matters to personnel selection, from reference service to automation. It is well illustrated and gives a well-rounded presentation.

A few books on the administration of technical libraries at universities have been written in the past few years, but their emphasis is on British practice. The treatment tends to be rather general, with not much emphasis on technical libraries, as illustrated by one work.[4]

Budgets

Even the wealthiest of universities must prepare and adhere to a budget. In the case of schools which are not in the diminishing ranks of the well-to-do institutions, budgets are of crucial importance. The size of a university library budget can mean the difference between adequate funding for the year (most budgets are prepared on an annual basis) and a period of hardship and inadequacies. When funds are abundant, budgets are loosely drawn up, with room for emergencies and unexpected expenditures. But in recent years most university budgets have been carefully scrutinized, and because of tighter funds for universities in the United States, both public and private, items are being cut down or eliminated whenever possible. Most libraries can tolerate some reduction, but beyond that the proper functioning and effectiveness of the system are put in jeopardy. Since the source of funds is beyond the control of the heads of library systems, the most they can do is to present convincing figures and descriptions of their needs to university administrations, then await the annual competition for funds with other university units. While no university could possibly allow its library system to close, many campus administrators do not have a clear idea of the importance of university libraries and prune budget requests accordingly. Other administrators may appreciate the value of the library but have no means of providing adequate budgets. This is a period when libraries could well use "friends of the library" in the form of faculty members willing to speak up for library needs, but in these days of tight restrictions on funds this sort of support is often hard to find.

In a well-run library system the process of preparing the budget includes receiving, through administrative channels, estimations from each library unit as to its needs for the coming year. While current restrictions preclude granting each library unit all the funds it might want, the process of soliciting comments from unit heads is still proper and useful. Extreme hardships come to light, with some measure of relief at least a possibility. With no input, library directors may be unaware of serious deficiencies in funds. Most budgets are started months before the university trustees finally act on them, as it is a detailed, laborious process, both for the library administration and for the university as a whole.

In a science division, the division head or head of the group is responsible for getting requests from each unit head, then refining them before sending them up the administrative ladder. Funds for staffing as well as for literature and equipment are involved in budget making.

In times of low budgets most library systems are usually reluctant to add new positions to any unit. The unit head and the supervisors above that person must have a solid case if they can hope to succeed. The costs of a staff member are not restricted to salaries alone; they include a fair amount of fringe benefits, such as health care, pension costs for certain professionals, holiday and vacation pay—all of which add up to a significant portion of the library budget. It should be no surprise then that administrators stress the need to keep staff sizes to a minimum. Naturally a minimum staff must be kept on hand, but whether a given position is really necessary is a worry that budget makers constantly have on their minds. Besides the annual increases that nonunion employees are granted, based on formulas worked out by the university administration, there are also the increases mandated by union contracts, which leave no room for reducing increases to fit the current financial standings of the university. In a large system it is not unusual that an additional quarter of a million dollars, or more, will be set aside per year just to cover union members' increases. To keep salaries equitable in the system, the others—the nonunion members—must also be granted reasonable increases. Another annual pressure for increased salaries is the steady increase in starting salaries for those just graduating from library schools. Lately, with the increased costs of living each year, this figure has risen three or four hundred dollars per year. Even student hourly rates go up a bit each year. Federal minimums for such hourly workers will keep the pressure on to increase their pay scales further.

Based on data for six large university libraries for the period 1968-1969 to 1972-1973, the budgets of research libraries will show the following rough averages of percentages of budgets spent for staffing, collections, and miscellany.[5]

Literature and binding	29.4%
Salaries	60.3%
Other operating expenses	10.3%

The need to keep salaries reasonable makes steady inroads on the amount of funding left for literature and binding. The problem of providing adequate collections is complicated further by price increases of books in recent years. Part of this is being caused by the normal increase in labor and materials in the publishing industry, but it is compounded by the devaluation of the dollar, which has caused foreign materials to shoot up in price for libraries in the United States.

Another cost factor, which affects science and engineering libraries more than those serving other disciplines, is the marked increase in price of periodicals, which are so important in technical libraries. While book price increases have been significant, periodical increases have been larger.

In regard to book prices, the 1973 average prices for monographs shows that sci-tech books lead in this regard, as listed below:[6]

Average price, all disciplines	$12.20
Science	17.34
Technology	15.38

An informal survey of dozens of science books being considered for purchase at Columbia University in early 1974 showed average prices to be still higher than the above figures—closer to $20 each. The 1973 survey perhaps included some popular works on science not of interest to universities, thus making books for the campus libraries in these disciplines even more costly than the table indicates.

When the average sci-tech librarian receives no increase in funds, or only a moderate increase, he has a real dilemma. The amount of material purchased must be reduced in order to stretch the budget, yet the demands made on the library do not diminish. In fact, enrollments in some subjects, such as psychology, life sciences, and engineering, seem to be increasing now, making the budget crunch even worse. New journals are constantly appearing on the scene, many of which are essential. In order to buy the new ones, some journals must be cancelled and the number of monographs purchased each year must be reduced. Some university sci-tech libraries have little money left for monographs after paying for subscriptions and buying books required by professors for assigned readings. This is, of course, an unfortunate situation, as no collection can maintain its usefulness for long without a reasonable number of monographs, even in sci-tech libraries where journals are of prime importance. Books still play a big part in any technical collection.

The funds for binding should be based upon the number of titles required to be bound, which can often be fewer than the number of subscriptions. Each library, especially in a decentralized organization, generally receives journals duplicated elsewhere on a campus, although there is great pressure on most librarians to keep this practice to a minimum now. Also, many titles of ephemeral interest may well be worth having a subscription to, but may not necessarily require binding. A good library system is constantly searching for cheaper ways to bind journals, as long as the method chosen matches the probable degree of use of the journal. Some titles, such as *Chemical Abstracts* in a chemistry library, require the best binding possible, but titles that are little used can be satisfactorily bound by cheaper methods—for example, allowing only one color and not permitting expensive extras like maps or foldout drawings.

Another element in the budget concerns equipment and supplies. In some libraries the individual unit has no separate budget for these items; rather only one lump sum is allotted for the entire library system. This is generally satisfactory, since on one hand it is too cumbersome to establish a separate budget for each library unit for small items such as pencils and paper clips, and, on the other hand, equipment tends to be so expensive that dividing limited funds up into too many units could result in some libraries being allotted enough for only half a typewriter or a portion of the cost of a new microform reader-printer. By lumping such funds under one administrator for the entire library system, the amount on hand becomes substantial enough to allow some libraries to be granted new pieces of equipment, even if all requests cannot be handled each year. To determine the needs, it is customary to ask each unit head to prepare a list of requirements before budgets are ready for allocation and use; items are arranged by the division head or group administrator on a priority basis, before submission to the library administrator responsible for spending that budget.

Each library unit should be informed of its total budgets for staff and for literature and binding early in the new fiscal year, which is often on a July-through-June basis. While unit heads and their supervisors have submitted budget requests up through channels, the final choice is usually up to the director or one of his assistants, and to the head of personnel and the administrator responsible for managing funds for literature and binding. An overall look at requests of smaller units—both in order to be consistent and to have data on all the factors that go into a decision on a budget—is essential.

Well-run systems provide at least monthly budgetary statements, showing amounts spent, names of vendors, and balances and amounts set aside for material on order but not yet billed. This process, called encumbering funds, is essential so that invoices do not appear later, long after the material was ordered, with no money put aside to cover them. The same principle holds for periodical subscriptions: the one in charge of the budget may have to announce a moratorium on the purchase of more books late in the budget year if periodical subscription invoices are still to be paid.

Figure 1 shows a typical monthly statement for the literature and binding funds for a unit library. It is computer-printed and normally appears early in a new month. Some pages list the names of vendors and invoice numbers, so that if desired, it is possible to check back to find out exactly what each charge is for. It is customary for a central library unit to pay bills, once departmental units check the invoices and approve them for payment. The exception is monograph orders, which are more cut and dried matters, requiring no further checking.

Funds for continuations refer to items that are issued in irregular parts, such as multivolumed encyclopedias issued volume by volume. Sometimes annuals or the ''advances in . . .'' types of serials are placed in this category.

Besides a regular budget, libraries sometimes receive special funds in the form of gifts, perhaps from donors interested in furthering a certain

PHYSICS

FUND	ACCOUNT NO.	NAME OF ACCOUNT	BALANCE	ALLOCATION	INCOME	EXPENDITURE	ENCUMBRANCE
740	51083700005	ASTRONOMY BOOKS	547.17CR	600.00CR	461.72CR	284.78	225.77
741	51083700005	ASTRONOMY PERIODICALS	2,825.57CR	3,200.00CR	.00	374.03	.00
742	51083700005	ASTRONOMY CONTINUATIONS	.00*	.00	.00	.00	.00
745	51083700005	PHYSICS BOOKS	1,650.91CR	2,500.00CR	1,415.33CR	954.07	1,310.35
746	51083700005	PHYSICS PERIODICALS	15,209.12CR	15,700.00CR	6.00CR	490.88	6.00
747	51083700005	PHYSICS CONTINUATIONS	1,501.55CR	2,000.00CR	.00	498.45	.00
1745	51083700005	PHYSICS BINDING	1,566.95CR	1,700.00CR	.00	133.05	.00

EXPENDITURE STATEMENT   FOR PERIOD ENDING SEPTEMBER 30, 1974

745   PHYSICS BOOKS   PHYSICS   51083700005

CHECK	DESCRIPTION	BALANCE	ALLOCATION	INCOME	EXPENDITURE	ENCUMBRANCE
	BALANCE FORWARD:	1,997.79CR	2,500.00CR	1,415.33CR	437.02	1,480.52
L67029	YANKEE BOOK PEDDLER, INC.				10.35	
L67033	RICHARD ABEL & COMPANY, INC.				40.24	
L67146	RICHARD ABEL & COMPANY, INC.				13.03	
L67149	ACADEMIC PRESS, INC.				18.00	
L67223	W. A. SANDERS CO.				21.95	
L67241	RICHARD ABEL & COMPANY, INC.				17.41	
L67313	RICHARD ABEL & CANY, INC.				48.07	
L67316	AMERICAN INSTITUTE OF PHYSICS				19.50	
L67372	MARTINUS NIJHOFF				30.40	
L67372	MARTINUS NIJHOFF				30.40	
L67372	MARTINUS NIJHOFF				30.40	
L67393	YANKEE BOOK PEDDLER, INC.				2.02	
L67459	SPRINGER VERLAG, NEW YORK, INC				34.02	
L67459	SPRINGER VERLAG, NEW YORK, INC				34.02	
L67464	SPRINGER VERLAG, NEW YORK, INC				34.02	
L67479	JOHN WILEY & SONS INC.				15.25	
L67483	YANKEE BOOK PEDDLER, INC.				30.38	
L67483	YANKEE BOOK PEDDLER, INC.				2.65	
L67483	YANKEE BOOK PEDDLER, INC.				30.38	
L67483	YANKEE BOOK PEDDLER, INC.				2.65	
L67483	YANKEE BOOK PEDDLER, INC.				30.38	
L67483	YANKEE BOOK PEDDLER, INC.				2.65	
L67653	OXFORD UNIVERSITY PRESS, INC.				14.88	
	TOTAL ENCUMBRANCE LAST MONTH					1,480.52
	TOTAL ENCUMBRANCE THIS MONTH					1,310.35
	CURRENT BALANCE	1,650.91CR	2,500.00CR	1,415.33CR	954.07	1,310.35

Figure 1 Monthly financial statement printout

library. While this is usually an irregular type of bonus, a few libraries are fortunate to have regular income from wills, special funds, and the like, to add to their budgets. A few legendary university units are so well endowed that they do not even require a budget from the library system. Unfortunately, such cases are few and far between.

A useful collection of papers describing specific studies on cost reduction, as well as a literature review and some general studies, was edited by Slater.[7] There is great emphasis on the use of computers in the specific cases reported.

Planning and Systems Analysis

One of the traditional duties of an administrator is to make plans for the operations supervised. Short-range planning, valuable as that may be, is not enough; someone must take a long-range look at things as well. While an individual library unit is seldom asked to make long-range plans on its own, it is not unusual for a division head or a group administrator to be asked to prepare such plans for the library administration. Shorter-range planning is often done by a unit head, subject to review by the supervisor.

Typical topics for short-range planning projects could range from estimates of collection growth in the next year to a revision of a layout of a library unit. Long-range planning might well involve an estimate of the types of future computer services required or the best ways to popularize an instructional program with faculty members in the next five to ten years. While planning is still not a science, certain principles are valid. One of them is that one's personal bias should not hold sway, a situation fatal to accurate planning. Another is the need for basing decisions on the best data available, checking and double-checking all "facts" whenever possible. A third principle might well be to get the opinions of persons with special skills if the planner is in unfamiliar territory. No one can be expected to be equally well versed in every field, so librarians working on a topic new to them should not be reluctant to seek outside aid.

Some of the larger library systems have established a separate planning section in order to systematize the process of making plans. This section usually reports directly to the director of libraries, as its plans generally originate at the director's request. The unit should, of course, also be available to advise various librarians within the system who need skilled help in the methodology of certain plans or surveys. Ideally the head of such a unit should have a library degree, as well as experience and training in systems analysis, computer operation and programming, and budgetary matters.

Systems analysis is one of the main techniques used by skilled planners. While it can apply to almost any organization, the actual techniques to be used for an application can vary from situation to situation.

A great deal has been written about systems analysis, with more and more of it oriented toward librarians and information scientists. "Systems analysis" may sound quite esoteric and complicated, but, in many ways, it is merely a name for good management techniques. In the words of Edythe Moore, "systems analysis is no more than organized common sense, an organized approach to problem-solving and the use of the management engineering tools and techniques that have been available to the business community for many years."[8] She goes on to point out that librarians need to apply these techniques to their own organizations. Other articles in the February 1967 issue of *Special Libraries* describe specific applications of systems analysis to libraries. In a later article for the novice in systems work, Burns describes its characteristics and applications.[9]

The processes involved in systems analysis are described by Paul Fasana, who states that the first objective of the systems analyst must be to get a picture of an entire system. The second objective, he says, is to compare the objectives of the organization with its actual accomplishments.[10] Often this is done in terms of unit costs, such as the average total cost of cataloging a book. Once problems are identified, the systems analyst works with management to determine which areas should be given further attention. He candidly states that "systems analysis is an art based on rather gross, primarily quantitative techniques," and that it cannot be 100 percent objective. The costs are often high, and the process can be time-consuming, he points out. Despite these limitations, he sees it as a means of systematic analysis that he recommends for library use. He defines systems analysis as "a discipline which is presently attempting to synthesize previous theories and branches of management science into a new discipline."

Other articles following Fasana's in the *Library Trends* issue give examples of the use of systems analysis, and implementation of the changes called for, in various library situations.

Closely related to systems analysis, yet perhaps even more complex sounding to the uninitiated, is the process called operations research. It developed as a discipline during World War II, serving as a scientific means of solving military problems. Since then it has been applied to business, industry, and many other areas. Ferdinand Leimkuhler indicated its close relationship to systems analysis by the following definition: "Operations research is the art of using the scientific method to help understand and solve sociotechnical problems."[11] This journal issue also contains accounts of the application of operations research to research libraries, including a university library.

An application to libraries of one of the newer management techniques known as management by objectives, has been described in an article by Johnson.[12] He defines this technique as one which concentrates on arriving at a precise definition of the objectives, then on establishing a realistic plan for accomplishing the tasks, and finally on evaluating performance in measured results. As an example he cites a project for the reclassification of serials in a library.

It is apparent that science and engineering libraries need not be administered by haphazard principles, with unsolved problems of a managerial nature hanging over them for years. A careful application of systems analysis and operations research techniques should be made, after the library administration gives its approval to a request for these techniques by the division head or group administrator. Librarians must be just as scientific and modern in their roles as managers as their counterparts in business or industry are. The size and scope of a problem determine the probable cost and time required for a careful analysis. The more complicated the problem the more important it is to have the full backing and approval of the library administration.

Library Reports and Statistics

One requirement for a well-managed library is that the person in charge must have a good grasp of what is taking place in that unit, with some fair degree of accuracy. It is not enough to merely "feel" that certain things are taking place, or that other activities are not taking place. What is needed is a system for gathering facts on important aspects of an operation.

The only way to get valuable data is through the gathering of statistics and a system of reports. In the past some libraries have erred on the side of spending too much time and effort on gathering useless statistics, thus making the whole practice of collecting data suspect. But when done with wisdom and common sense, the process need not be burdensome and can provide invaluable data. For example, although the traditional circulation figures for libraries do not tell the entire story of how much use is made of the collections, they are nevertheless very useful measures of reader activity. One could overanalyze such figures, such as trying to determine with great precision the exact hour during the day at which the peak load of circulation occurs. It is probably accurate enough to observe casually that more students are on hand from noon to six P.M., except on weekends, compared to other hours of the day. On the other hand, it might be necessary to make a precise count of how many people use a library each hour on Saturdays to see if a reduction of hours on such days would be feasible. Judgment is required to decide what data are needed and what are not required.

Merely gathering data is not enough, as someone must analyze the facts, then prepare reports for appropriate library administrators. Reports may be periodic, such as weekly or monthly, or special one-time studies may be made. The most common reports for sci-tech libraries are as follows:

Circulation—data gathered daily, but summarized in report form monthly

Photocopy activities—same as circulation

Interlibrary loans—same as circulation

Inventories—usually done on an annual basis, if not less frequently, unless special problems call for more frequent studies of selected portions of a collection.

Number of patrons—usually done on a special basis, as circumstances require, such as hourly during the evenings or on the weekends.

General summaries—usually done on an annual basis, as part of a system-wide practice

When setting up a system of gathering statistics, it is important to review the need for it periodically, so that employees do not faithfully gather data long after the need to do so has ended.

Some library problems do not lend themselves to a statistical study, particularly if they involve personnel problems, faculty opinions, or other topics traditionally difficult to measure quantitatively. In such cases, the writers of reports must make every attempt to be unbiased in their reports and to bring out all elements of the situation as fairly as possible. If this is done, the chances that a wise, fair decision will be made are much greater than if tradition, personal bias, or indifference to another's viewpoint are allowed to control the process of decision-making.

At universities where government contracts account for a significant portion of the total funding, it is occasionally required that the federal government be provided with data on the relationship of research to instructional costs within the university library system. This is needed for computing overhead rates for those working on research contracts. Although at most universities the science, engineering, and medical departments tend to have the most contracts, the government has been willing to accept an overall average of research costs for the entire library system rather than require separate figures for the technical libraries. Of course, many factors enter into a study of this sort, ranging from the types of literature required for research to the kinds of reference service needed by researchers. A study at Columbia University to determine the ratio of costs required to support research versus those for supporting the library system involved several types of data gathering and cut across the entire library system.[13] The project, which took place over a twelve-month period, revealed many interesting bits of data as byproducts of the project.

Libraries which receive governmental or private grants are almost always required to make periodic reports on the use of funds and on progress toward the goals of the funded project. Annual reports are the most common type for this purpose; a final report is made upon completion of the project. Librarians should be alert to possible sources of funds for this purpose, since local funds are rarely adequate for research projects of any size.

Still another type of report useful in sci-tech libraries is the trip report, written by a staff member upon return from a conference, seminar, or the like. When circulated within a science division, it serves to educate all staff members and keep them updated on new developments. Some may be of broad enough interest to warrant circulating them to a wider circle within the library system. More than one library system has a newsletter in which such accounts of meetings are summarized.

Notes

[1] Louis Round Wilson and Maurice F. Tauber, *The University Library: The Organization, Administration and Functions of Academic Libraries*, 2d ed. (New York: Columbia University Press, 1956), 641 p. (The third edition is in preparation.)

[2] Guy R. Lyle, *The Administration of the College Library*, 4th ed. (New York: Wilson, 1974), 320 p.

[3] R. D. Rogers and D. C. Weber. *University Library Administration* (New York: Wilson, 1971), 454 p.

[4] D. L. Smith and E. O. Baxter, *College Library Administration in Colleges of Technology, Art, Commerce and Further Education* (New York: Oxford, 1965), 185 p. G. A. Thompson, ed., *The Technical College Library: A Primer for Its Development* (London: Deutsch, 1969), 135 p.

[5] Association of Research Libraries, *Academic Library Statistics* (Washington, D.C.: 1968/1969-1972/1973).

[6] "1973: U.S. Book Industry Statistics: Titles, Prices, Sales Trends," *Publishers Weekly* 205, no. 5 (February 4, 1974): 53, 56-58.

[7] Frank Slater, ed., *Cost Reduction for Special Libraries and Information Centers* (Washington, D.C.: American Society for Information Science, 1973), 187 p.

[8] Edythe Moore, "Systems Analysis: An Overview," *Special Libraries* 58, no. 2 (February 1967): 87-90.

[9] Robert W. Burns, Jr., "A Generalized Methodology for Library Systems Analysis," *College & Research Libraries* 32, no. 4 (July 1971): 295-303.

[10] Paul J. Fasana, "Systems Analysis." In F. Wilfred Lancaster, ed., "Systems Design and Analysis for Libraries," *Library Trends* 21, no. 4 (April 1973): 465-478.

[11] Ferdinand F. Leimkuhler, "Library Operations Research: A Process of Discovery and Justification." In "Operations Research: Implications for Libraries. Proceedings of the 35th Annual Conference of the Graduate Library School [University of Chicago], August 2-4, 1971," *Library Quarterly* 42, no. 1 (January 1972): 84-96.

[12] Edward R. Johnson, "Applying 'Management by Objectives' to the University Library," *College & Research Libraries* 34, no. 6 (November 1973): 436-439.

[13] Ellis Mount and Paul Fasana, "An Approach to the Measurement of Use and Cost of a Large Academic Research Library System: A Report of a Study Done at Columbia University Libraries," *College & Research Libraries* 33, no. 3 (May 1972): 199-211.

4

Staffing and Personnel Management

The quality of library service is clearly dependent to a great extent upon the quality of the staff—its background, training, motivation, and experience. The size of the staff is also extremely important. This chapter will describe the work of persons involved in science and engineering libraries at various levels, ranging from administrative and supervisory levels to part-time student help. The qualifications, duties, and working conditions for all such employees, along with the training and evaluation of employees, will be discussed.

Supervisory and Administrative Positions

Most science and engineering libraries at universities are either organized in a divisional plan, supervised by the division head, or else are in a grouping of public service units reporting to a librarian who is probably an assistant director. The larger the library system, the more likely it will have a divisional arrangement, as it would be cumbersome for several dozen departmental libraries to report to one person. Smaller systems seem to manage with all departmental library heads reporting to one person, but perhaps a maximum of only eight to ten units would be involved in such cases.

In the divisional plan, the fact that each division is oriented toward certain disciplines, such as science and engineering, increases the likelihood that first choice for such posts would go to librarians with suitable subject backgrounds and experience. Normally, a degree in science or engineering, plus library science, is the minimum educational requirement for such a position; several years of pertinent experience are also required. It is not unusual for division heads to have a master's degree in science or engineering. Anything less than a bachelor's degree would be a real handicap in view of the specialized nature of the collections and services involved in such a division.

The division head is responsible for long-range planning, coordination of budgetary data, supervision of the professional librarians in the various units, and general liaison between that division and the rest of the library system and outside contacts. Many in this post also have final approval over purchases of literature for the division.

Division heads may report to an assistant director or to the director, depending upon many factors, one of which is the total number of divisions. The larger the number, the more unlikely that all will report directly to the director; hence the need for an assistant director to have this responsibility.

In regard to the librarians responsible for the individual library units, once again the type of organization has much to do with the number and responsibilities of such positions. If there is a consolidated plan, with only one physical unit, the head of the science-engineering division or grouping normally has his office in that building, and assigns specific duties to other librarians, such as reference service, collection development, or use of computers and automation. This allows the librarians to develop skills in that specialty and to develop programs that require a concerted effort rather than spasmodic attention. It also allows a bit more leeway in the event of absences and vacations since a centralized library might have as many as six professionals on the staff.

In the case of decentralized libraries, one or more units are assigned as the responsibility of each librarian. There the librarian has to know all aspects of the job—reference, supervision of the staff, collection development techniques, etc. Liaison with the faculty and other users served is another responsibility.

If a given unit is too large for this arrangement, two or more librarians may be required to operate and supervise it. Another plan is for the division head to be responsible not only for the division but also for one of the units within it. In such cases, the unit involved is usually the largest one, and one or more assistant librarians may be necessary.

In most universities today a master's degree in library science or information science, together with the appropriate collegiate subject training, is required for a professional position. Some, such as the City University of New York, require either a master's degree in a subject (plus the library degree) or evidence that the incumbent is enrolled in such a program, with retention dependent upon gaining that degree. Once in a while in an emergency, a person in library school with exceptional skills may be hired on a part-time basis with the agreement that a permanent position will depend upon completing the library degree requirements in a given time. Such arrangements are usually held to a minimum, however.

The survey I made in 1972 of twenty-two universities included a study of the backgrounds of sixty-seven librarians working in science-engineering libraries.[1] As expected, a high percentage—93 percent—had a library degree. Sometimes librarians in such libraries have been previously employed in laboratories or in teaching sciences; indeed the survey revealed that 17 percent of them had had prior work experience in the sciences or engineering. The following table shows their educational background in science or engineering:

Sci-Tech Training

	Pct.
No collegiate training	24
Some, but no degree	30
Bachelor's degree	22
Master's degree	20
Doctorate degree	1
No data supplied	3

Almost three-fourths of the librarians had had collegiate-level training in science or engineering, and nearly half had degrees in these fields.

In regard to utilization of their training and background, 35 percent felt that their present position made full utilization of their background, while 62 percent felt that it was only partially utilized. Nevertheless, many library systems are now increasingly attempting to make better use of their librarians' training and experience, since there appears to be room for improvement at most universities, as shown by these figures. Surprisingly, however, the degree of unrest caused by nonutilization of background was not extensive: 50 percent of them said they were very satisfied with their positions and 42 percent said they were reasonably satisfied.

Librarians must weigh the advantages and disadvantages of working conditions offered in various types of libraries. In the 1972 survey mentioned previously, the university sci-tech librarians interviewed stated that what they most liked about their work was their professional duties; salaries were near the end of thelist. As causes of dissatisfaction, physical facilities and types of duties were ranked higher than salaries. So for some librarians the type of work assignments was seen as both the source of the greatest satisfaction and the greatest dissatisfaction.

Another factor which has entered the educational library picture is the question of tenure for librarians. In some library systems librarians have status comparable to faculty members, and are also subject to the rules governing tenure. To qualify for a higher ranking, they must compete with professors also seeking tenure, which, to many librarians, is not a desirable situation. Some universities, on the other hand, treat librarians as neither faculty nor administration, but as a separate class—librarians. This is more often true in some of the larger systems, where there may be one hundred librarians or more, enough to make it worthwhile to have separate treatment for a group of that size. Tallau and Beede wrote an article recommending that librarians form their own faculty rather than try to join the academic faculty.[2] A very comprehensive annotated bibliography on faculty status for librarians, containing over two hundred items, was compiled by Huling.[3]

An article by Holley describes many administrative problems which have emerged in recent years, including the organizational arrangements for librarians as contrasted with the faculty (faculty status, tenure, etc.), the outlook for unions, participatory management, and systems of promoting librarians. These topics apply to most universities, and not merely to urban universities as the title implies.[4] In regard to unionization of library staffs, many of the most comprehensive articles appear to have been written a few years ago, perhaps when the issue was newer. One of these was Nyren's survey of union activities at several types of libraries, including academic.[5] Hopkins gave a slightly more recent survey of union events and their probable causes, concluding with a sizable bibliography.[6] Two articles by Weatherford describe findings of a survey of collective bargaining in academic libraries.[7] Unionization is a controversial topic, usually arousing strong feelings in librarians for or against.

Nonsupervisory Professional Positions

In decentralized library systems, most sci-tech librarians supervise a small or even medium-sized library unit. The exceptions are those universities with some rather large units among their technical libraries. In the latter case, some librarians may hold staff positions, such as assistant librarian for the engineering library, or head of reference work for the biomedical library. Such positions involve only minimal supervision. They are more apt to involve responsibility for supervision of a portion of a unit, such as the supporting staff required for circulation and physical care of the collection.

In consolidated systems, where there may be only one or two physical units, the amount of supervision—the number of people supervised—is generally the same as in decentralized units. Again, however, the scope of the supervision is usually restricted to one aspect of the library, such as reference or SDI service. The head of the science-engineering division or center, as it may be called, may then be the only employee responsible for a complete library unit.

Some librarians relish responsibility for all aspects of a library unit, while others prefer the more specialized role found in consolidated units. A lot depends upon the personal preference of the librarian, as is true for almost any position. The constant parade of a variety of problems, ranging from coping with broken microfilm readers to faculty requests for quick reference service, is a challenge to some librarians. Others prefer not to be "jacks-of-all-trades" so that they can concentrate on developing certain projects and goals.

Another nonsupervisory position, somewhat recent in origin, is that of a science bibliographer or collection officer, who is primarily responsible for establishing collection development policies, making selections, weeding the collections, and evaluating gifts. This sort of position may be found in either a decentralized or a consolidated organization. The incumbents must possess good backgrounds in the subject areas they cover.

Supporting Staffs and Part-time Employees

The duties of full-time employees who are not in professional positions may consist of the following: responsibility for the operation of the circulation section of a moderately large unit; performance of clerical functions (filing, typing, checking in journals, preparing journals for the bindery, or any of a variety of similar tasks); response to simple reference questions, even some on a moderately complex level, or referring more complicated queries to the professional staff.

Many of these employees have bachelor's degrees (or sometimes higher degrees), or else are working towards a degree by taking one or two courses per semester, often at no charge for tuition. Consequently, their educational level is generally higher than that of their counterparts in noneducational libraries. Tuition exemption is a very attractive feature of these jobs, often bringing in highly motivated employees. Universities with library schools have an extra bonus in that many library employees are enrolled in such programs and thus have even higher interest in their jobs and sometimes bring previous library experience to the job. There are exceptions, of course, and some of the supporting staff members either do not pass probation or do so by a narrow margin. (Most universities have a probationary period of six months to a year for professional librarians and two months for supporting staff.)

At some institutions librarians have been approached for unionization purposes, but the majority of professionals are not yet involved. In more and more schools, however, the supporting staff belongs to a union, usually being required to join after passing probation. There are pros and cons on such matters. It is no doubt true that clerical salaries are, on the average, higher at institutions with a clerical union, but along with benefits come restrictions, such as emphasis on seniority for consideration for higher-ranking jobs and required union dues. Librarians at universities will no doubt be working with unionized supporting-staff members in many institutions from now on.

The other component of the nonprofessional work force at most schools is the part-time student, without whose help most college and university libraries would be in dire straits. Students are available to work evenings or weekends as well as during the week at all hours. Their work ranges from simple book shelving and shelf-reading to checking in journals, mending books, typing, filing, and a host of other clerical tasks vital to the operation of any library. Some of these students are extremely conscientious and bright, and only a few turn out to be indifferent and listless. One has to expect them to work fewer hours during mid-term and final examinations, but in general they provide a very important service at university libraries.

Most of them are paid weekly, working at hourly rates. If there are union jobs at a given library, care must be taken not to eliminate a union job in favor of student help without an agreement with the union. Likewise, students do have to take time for their studies, so their work schedules are usually at the mercy of their class schedules. At times it seems that every student who wants to work has classes in the mornings or on certain afternoons. However, some are available during vacations and other intersession periods, which become good times to catch up on projects that somehow never seem to get done while school is in session.

Staff Sizes

As discussed previously, the number of professional librarians per sci-tech unit is largely a function of the size of the unit and of the type of organization used. In a centralized unit it is not uncommon to have six or more professionals assigned there, whereas in a decentralized system there is seldom more than one professional librarian per unit, or in the case of small units, even one-half librarian per unit. Moderate-sized units in decentralized systems may have two or three professionals, with one in charge of the unit and the others given assignments such as reference librarian or technical services librarian or responsibility for collection development. If there is only one professional in addition to the head of the unit, the second spot is usually designated as assistant librarian, with incumbents having wide responsibilities to share with the unit head.

In most universities all cataloging and placing of orders is done in central units in the main library building; hence, few sci-tech library units have their own cataloger. One exception is the engineering and mathematical sciences library at UCLA, where three technical services librarians are on duty, doing all the cataloging for the unit.

In small units there may be only one full-time supporting-staff person assigned, or perhaps two if work loads justify it. In such cases there is a one-to-one ratio of supporting-staff positions to professionals, much lower than the average for the typical university library system. At the Columbia University Library, for example, there are around 130 professionals and 230 supporting staff positions, plus around 35 staff members in supervisory positions, programming operations, and secretarial positions.

Most library systems are trying to increase the ratio of nonprofessional to professional positions for at least two reasons. One is to reduce costs—a commendable reason as long as service is not impaired significantly as a result. The other reason is to make professional positions more challenging by eliminating those which are not really full-time jobs. Regardless of whether librarians may be relatively more abundant or scarce to hire, it does the profession no good if a library has positions which do not contain enough professional-level duties to make them interesting. It is a waste of university money and of the incumbent's time. The trend is definitely toward careful reevaluation of jobs from this point of view.

Consolidated libraries are likely to have a higher ratio of nonprofessional to professional jobs simply because few small units require a full-time or part-time librarian to supervise them. If a system consolidated ten units, each having one librarian in charge, into one unit, it would not be unusual if five or six librarians might suffice in the new unit. However, the number of nonprofessionals might actually increase since the tendency is to increase the hours the library is open when consolidation takes place.

As for part-time help, it is not uncommon for a small unit to have five to ten part-time students on its roster, each working around ten to fifteen hours a week. Larger units may have a score or more students, depending, of course, on the actual size of the unit. They usually make good employees but often overestimate the amount of time they can work. Thus wise librarians often overhire at the beginning of a term in anticipation of the inevitable decrease in weekly hours the staff works as the term wears on. A well-knit group of sci-tech libraries should compile a list of available part-time employees, showing the hours available for an occasional emergency stint, with students able to work in any unit in the group. It will prove to be invaluable when students wait until the last minute to announce their unavailability for work.

Hiring Practices

After the appropriate supervisory and administrative librarians have conducted interviews, the personnel office of the library system traditionally hires professional librarians. In divisional systems, this includes the division head. If the units report to an assistant director, this person is also involved. In some libraries the director also interviews each professional candidate.

Governmental and university practices now make it almost mandatory to advertise new positions to the general public as well as to the existing staff. With the greater care taken not to discriminate on the basis of age, race, sex, or religion, hiring practices have become fairer than in previous years. At one time positions in a library system were often awarded to persons on the staff with no formal announcements of the vacancy made to the staff or outside the library. This led to morale problems for staff members wishing to advance themselves. There was discrimination of various kinds, although not admitted, and minority group members were seldom given much of a chance at a position. So the changes in hiring policies are welcomed by all who have sought to improve this phase of librarianship. Though total reform has not been achieved, the improvement is significant.

Besides advertisements in newspapers or in library journals, other sources for applicants are library schools and library conferences at which placement services are offered. The most important positions often rely on word-of-mouth communication in the profession, which is not unethical as long as public announcement is also made. Search committees are often used for important posts; these committees evaluate candidates and make recommendations to the director of libraries, who makes the final selection.

During interviews most supervisors try to measure up the applicant to what the job requires. A perfect match of experience and/or training is hard to find, and interviewers are usually willing to give up a bit on ideal requirements if the applicant seems to bring intelligence, enthusiasm, and a pleasant personality to the job. More than one person with a perfect background of technical requirements, such as the exact degree required or type of experience wanted, has been passed over because his or her record in school or in previous positions indicated a history of immaturity, indifference, or other qualities that would hamper a good performance in the position. On the other hand, requirements cannot be ignored, nor can too many exceptions be made; otherwise the posts would be filled with well-meaning but incompetent professionals. They may have an unpleasant experience if put into positions for which they are poorly suited, and everyone's time is wasted as replacements are eventually sought. It is the borderline applicant which gives the supervisory staff the most problems; the clearcut cases of suitability or unsuitability are easier to spot and to handle.

Starting salaries in university libraries vary greatly from one region or type of university to another. Most professional library associations make salary surveys on a relatively frequent basis; one example is the Special Libraries Association, which does so every few years. Its most recent survey is, as usual, more pertinent to nonuniversity positions, but it does serve as a guide to what is being currently paid.[8] This survey, taken in 1973, of nearly thirty-nine hundred special librarians, showed the average salary to be $14,000, with the mean at $12,800. Besides the breakdown of data by geographical region, age of librarian, and amount of experience, among other factors discussed, the figures for the type of position revealed a mean of $14,300 for general academic libraries, while the subject academic library paid a mean of $13,500. The figure for general academic libraries probably included top administrators, thus giving a higher average than the subject library, which probably includes many beginning librarians, who are paid at lower levels.

Another useful survey of salaries is that for recent graduates of library schools, which appears annually in *Library Journal.* In the most recent one Learmont and Frarey computed that the average for all 1973 graduates holding the master's degree, in beginning positions, was around $9,400.[9] Academic positions also averaged at this figure, while public library positions averaged about $9,000 and school library posts about $9,700.

Applicants should find out the probable salary range or minimum involved, although an exact figure is sometimes not given until a job is actually offered. Fringe benefits should also be inquired about.

In many universities librarians are hired on an annual basis, with re-hiring almost assured unless the person does not pass probation, which may last one or two years. In extreme cases of misfits, retention may be only for one year. Those who are not re-hired are generally given generous notice time.

The previously mentioned trend toward seeking faculty status and consequently tenure for librarians finds librarians on both sides of the issue. Those seeing it as primarily one of job security may gloss over the disadvantages of tenure quotas or competition with faculty for a limited number of tenured positions. Others feel that, while librarians definitely have a place in the instructional activities, their primary position is not that of a faculty person, and they prefer to seek recognition as a librarian.

Training and Evaluation of Staff Members

No matter how much previous experience a new employee on the library staff may have, whether it be a professional, a supporting-staff person, or a part-time student, there are obviously still many things to learn about a position in a new library. Training new employees in an efficient, competent manner is vital to the smooth operation of the unit, yet it is often done haphazardly.

Taking professionals first, there should be a written job description providing a reasonable degree of detail, which the supervisor or division head should discuss early on the first day. It is assumed that the applicants, when interviewed, are given the basic description of the duties. The written description is often used to prepare the sort of summary used for outside advertising and internal job postings, or to serve as the basis for initial discussion with applicants.

No job description, however, no matter how well written, is a substitute for proper training. A colleague, a supervisor—someone must assume the responsibility for showing a new employee the important parts of the job, introducing them to others with whom major contacts are made, and the like. The right start is extremely important.

If there are procedure manuals for the positions on the supporting staff, such write-ups are quite valuable for their supervisor to read. Lacking that, each person's duties must be listed and explained. The same holds for part-time positions; the professional librarians must have a good concept of their duties and responsibilities.

Each library system should have a written set of basic policies governing major aspects of professional positions, but not all are so equipped. These policies set forth the system's expectations of its librarians, its basic goals, and the major principles of the system.

In most libraries, new professionals serve a probationary period during which it is likely that they will not be earning their full salary for a portion of that time. Although that may sound disparaging, it is reasonable; for several months their value is apt to be on the minimal side. Some learn quickly and are soon running a library or performing staff duties very satisfactorily. Others may take six months or so to begin functioning smoothly at their work. It is a period for patience on the part of the supervisor, particularly if it is the professional's first position. More experienced librarians need a much shorter learning period. At the end of the probationary period, the supervisor prepares an evaluation of the employee, using prescribed forms provided for in the well-run library. In a good library system, this process of evaluation is repeated annually or biennially, so that employees are advised of their strong points and their weak ones, and given assistance in areas which need strengthening. For instance, this could be guidance in improving supervisory techniques, or study plans to develop stronger backgrounds in the subjects involved in their libraries. For a survey of performance appraisal techniques at over one hundred universities in the United States and Canada, the reader is referred to the study made by Johnson.[10] Annual reviews are made at 80 percent of the universities. Peer evaluation generally is considered very useful.

As for supporting-staff members, the type of records about their duties may depend a great deal upon two factors: the amount of initiative taken by the library administration just for the sake of good management or the existence of a union for supporting-staff members. If there is a clerical union, it is almost a prerequisite that there be written descriptions of the various classes of positions. It is not unusual for these jobs to exist in six or seven levels of pay rates, ranging from the simple messenger or page jobs to those requiring special skills and college backgrounds. Jobs are posted as vacancies occur, interested employees sign up, and then the most senior applicant in terms of union seniority or the one with the highest position (but lower ranking than the job opening) must be given a probationary period at the job. An exception would occur if a person lacked the stated requirements (such as foreign languages), or, if a test were involved, failed it (such as a typing test). Failure to perform satisfactorily during the probationary period, usually eight weeks, results in taking the next most qualified applicant. In the meantime the employee who fails probation is fitted back into a job at his or her former level.

During probation for supporting-staff members, whether unionized or not, the supervisors are expected to offer full help to employees in teaching them the job. In the absence of written job descriptions, much depends upon the memory of the supervisor as to what to teach. Since it is much more difficult to break in a new person in this way, the supervisor should work with his staff in compiling procedure manuals describing each job in considerable detail. Passing probation does not necessarily mean new employees have mastered all elements of a given job, but it does mean that they have shown an ability to master the job in a reasonable time, they have a good attitude towards a job, and they work well with the staff and/or the public.

Most libraries have a simple one- or two-page evaluation sheet to use for supporting-staff members, primarily to rank them at the end of the probation period or upon termination. Normally, they are not evaluated again unless they apply for a higher level job. Even though union contracts may restrict job evaluations to periods of probation or upon termination, employees and employers alike would benefit if informative job evaluations could be prepared for supporting-staff members more regularly, such as biennially, unless intervening job probationary periods exist. It allows the employee to know where he or she stands, and affords an opportunity for frank discussions between employer and employee.

In regard to part-time student employees, the records are simpler. Students do not normally belong to a union, and usually a simple evaluation sheet is used at the end of their first semester or term on the job. If their work is not satisfactory, they are not re-hired for another semester. The percentage who do not pass is quite small. As is the case with other jobs, there should be a certain amount of written material on hand for describing student jobs. Some duties, such as checking in serials, can be fairly complex, so that time spent in preparing written guidelines and procedures is well worth it. Some librarians give students informal tests in book shelving, card filing, or shelf-reading, once they have received instruction and have tried it briefly.

One of the great difficulties in maintaining good procedure manuals is to remember to update them as conditions and rules change. At the least, they must be reviewed before employees terminate their jobs. It is important to get their comments on the validity of the written manuals, then solicit their help in re-working portions, as required. Procedure manuals should never be thought of as sacred since no supervisor worthy of the name wants to instill a sense that nothing can be changed or improved in the organization. If that is the atmosphere, the supervisor is to blame if the employees in the unit lack initiative and if efficiency subsequently diminishes. What should be sought is a spirit of always trying to improve conditions or procedures. This does not obligate the supervisor to adopt each new proposal regardless of merit, but it does require open-mindedness to each suggestion. Those making suggestions should be made to feel that their ideas are appreciated, even when the proposed innovations may be totally unworkable. One never knows when an employee may come up with a very valuable idea. Suggestions from users should also be given encouragement and careful review.

The staffing of any organization is a serious matter since a library cannot give good service and maintain good collections without well-selected, well-trained staff members. It takes time to produce such a staff, but it is time very well spent.

Notes

[1]Ellis Mount, *University Science and Engineering Libraries—A Survey*, 1972, 26 p. (Available from ERIC Document Reproduction Service, Bethesda, Md. 20014, as ED 068 108.)

[2]Adeline Tallau and Benjamin R. Beede, "Faculty Status and Library Governance," *Library Journal* 99, no. 11 (June 1, 1974): 1521-1523.

[3]Nancy Huling, "Faculty Status—A Comprehensive Bibliography," *College & Research Libraries* 34, no. 6 (November 1973): 440-462.

[4]Edward G. Holley, "Organization and Administration of Urban University Libraries," *College & Research Libraries* 33, no. 3 (May 1972): 175-189.

[5]Karl Nyren, "Libraries and Labor Unions," *Library Journal* 92, no. 11 (June 1, 1967): 2115-2121.

[6]Joseph S. Hopkins, "Unions in Libraries," *Library Journal* 94, no. 17 (October 1, 1969): 3403-3407.

[7]John Weatherford, "Librarians in Faculty Unions," *Library Journal* 99, no. 17 (October 1, 1974): 2443-2446. John Weatherford, "Professional Associations and Bargaining Agents," *Library Journal* 100, no. 2 (January 15, 1975): 99-101.

[8]"SLA Salary Survey—1973," *Special Libraries* 64, no. 12 (December 1973): 594-628.

[9]Carlyle Frarey and Carol Learmont, "Placement and Salaries 1973: Not Much Change," *Library Journal* 99, no. 13 (July 1974): 1764-1774.

[10]Marjorie Johnson, "Performance Appraisal of Libraries—A Survey," *College & Research Libraries* 33, no. 5 (September 1972): 359-367.

5

Library Collections

Nature of Collections

The materials collected by a university library should reflect the instructional and research interests of the institution. There has never been any justification for a university library to build a strong collection in a subject of little or no interest to the school, either in its classroom work or its research areas. In these days of tight budgets and rising costs for literature, there is even less excuse for letting collection goals get out of step with local needs. Even so, this has happened in many institutions, and only the real budgetary problems most universities have been facing in recent years have forced librarians at such institutions to take a closer look at their collection policies and activities.

As stated above, most universities have two major levels of interest in subject areas: one is at the instructional level, which may range from undergraduate to graduate courses, which is in itself a considerable range to cover. The other level is that of research, whether it be research by doctoral candidates or by faculty members or by those on what is usually called the research staff. In the event doctoral degrees are not given in particular subjects, the chances are good that there would not be much faculty or staff research involving those subjects, although it can happen. As might be expected, many more requirements are placed on a university library when doctoral instruction and research are involved than when only undergraduate or master's level courses are offered. Both the size and complexity of the collection are affected.

The following portions of this section will describe what is required in sci-tech university collections for the university's different levels of need. It will be seen that there is a great difference between what is needed to support, for example, an undergraduate course in meteorology versus a doctoral program in that discipline.

Reserve Collections—One of the most basic parts of a university collection is that which is earmarked by the faculty as required reading, or perhaps, suggested reading, for their courses. This is so fundamental to the teaching program that a university library system is expected to supply it more or less automatically. In practice, however, a few exceptions may have to be made, such as when a professor may badly overestimate the number of works his class could hope to read, or when a professor expects an unreasonable number of copies of a particular work. Such exceptions have to be dealt with individually, and on a diplomatic basis.

The tendency for professors to overestimate the reading capacity of students seems more likely to occur in the humanities or social sciences than in sci-tech courses. Budgetary restrictions may make it necessary to refuse to get an inordinate number of new works for a given course or to get as many duplicate copies as some faculty members may deem necessary. On the average, five to six titles per course is typical for sci-tech courses, but exceptions are quite common. Some have more and some have less. As for the number of copies required, one rule of thumb is around fifteen to twenty students per copy, if it is required reading, but more can share a copy if the reading is optional, particularly if there are many other items on reserve for the course. Most libraries are reluctant to put a copy of a required text for the course on reserve, since students should be expected to have their own copies, and textbooks per se do not add much strength to a collection.

Reserve materials may vary from an entire monograph to a single chapter in a book, a periodical article, one entire issue of a journal, or a pamphlet. In a geology library it might be a map, or in a biology library a skeleton of a cat. Understandably, faculty members place much importance on having items in the library when the class is expected to read them. Nothing is more upsetting to a professor than to have the class report back that reserve materials are not on hand. Yet, in some cases, the professor is late in supplying the library with the list of reserve books (most libraries send out a form letter to all known faculty members a month or so before a semester begins in order to get lists back well before the new term), so that the library staff in such cases is not at fault. In some cases the material is available only from a foreign source, requiring several weeks of waiting. And too it is not unknown for professors to refer to works that have not even been published yet, selecting them on the basis of publishers' advertisements for works still in preparation. There are, of course, cases in which the library staff does not work efficiently and is to blame for items not being on hand when needed.

When periodical articles are to be placed on reserve, the question of copyrights comes up if photocopies are to be used. Some libraries hold stringently to the practice of making only one copy for a professor and making extra copies only if the publishers grant such privileges. Some publishers will give blanket permission, while others prefer to handle requests on an individual basis. As it is a time-consuming task for libraries, many of them pay no heed to it. The outlook for new legislation to cover this problem seems dim at this time, and it is difficult to predict what the new regulations will eventually be. Some professors make their own multiple copies, then turn them over to the library for reserve use. This may leave the library blameless legally, as far as copyright laws go, but it does nothing to solve the problem of fair photocopying procedures.

Material on reserve is usually given more stringent circulation rules, but this will be discussed more in the chapter on that subject.

Instructional Collections—If only undergraduate and first-year graduate instruction is offered in a subject, an adequate monograph collection would minimally consist of a reasonable number of English-language works in addition to the reserve material required. A few foreign-language titles may be in order, if there are landmark books on that subject in those languages. In addition, there should be a strong reference collection (including handbooks, encyclopedias, and dictionaries) pertaining to the subject. The journal holdings should include the major English-language titles, especially those of the recognized societies for that discipline. Most major societies in engineering and sciences are active in publishing journals, but the extent of activity varies tremendously from one organization to the next. One may issue only a single journal, while another may issue several dozen, all of which may be required in a library. For example, the Institute of Electrical and Electronics Engineers issues a general *Proceedings*, covering all aspects of this society's interests, plus a still more general journal, which includes news items (*IEEE Spectrum*). It also has over twenty technical groups within its membership, each issuing its own *Transactions.* So a library might well require all of their publications just to support instructional courses in electrical engineering up to the master's level.

A few basic journals covering science in general, such as *Science, Nature,* and *Scientific American,* are required. Foreign-language journals would rarely be required for instructional support, nor would journals devoted to the technician level be required. For example, journals on techniques of welding or the processing of leather would serve little purpose in most institutions teaching the traditional theoretical, basic courses in engineering. Only if such topics were taught, which is unlikely, would these journals be needed.

At least one good indexing or abstracting service for periodicals in the fields covered would be required for this level of a collection. Certain disciplines may require other items, such as maps (for geology courses), audiovisual aids (films or slides), or selected technical reports.

Research Collections—In order to support doctoral courses and dissertations, as well as independent research by the faculty and the research staff, a university library must have a much stronger, more complex collection of materials than for instructional support at the undergraduate and master's level. Monographs would have to include most advanced English works available with outstanding landmark volumes from foreign languages also represented. Proceedings of conferences, frequently expensive and hard to locate once they become out of print, must be on hand for appropriate subjects, as should the pertinent annual review series known by such titles as "Progress in . . ." or "Advances in . . . ." The reference collection would have to be more complete than for an instructional collection. But the periodicals, more than any other type of literature, would probably need the most strengthening. Major foreign-language journals would have to be included, and the English-language titles would have to be more numerous. Besides the major periodical abstracting and indexing service, other specialized ones applicable to the subject should be available. Reserve items must naturally be adequate. Related materials, such as maps and technical reports, would be important.

Summing it all up, the simplest way of expressing the difference between instructional collections and research collections is that the latter must have more depth, both in quantity and in intellectual treatment.

Research collections are obviously more expensive to build and maintain than instructional collections.

Minimal Collections—Many subjects are of little or no interest to a sci-tech library at a university. If there is no interest, and it is logical that there be no interest (e.g., not a case of local bias or temporary educational fads), then it is normal practice to avoid building a collection in such subjects. However, librarians should maintain small collections for topics of minor interest to a department, consisting of a few monographs, perhaps one journal, and a few major reference books.

In some cases a department may go through a period of several years during which minimum attention is given to research in a major portion of a discipline, perhaps because of the faculty's personal interests or the current emphasis in government contracts. In such a situation a librarian should alert the library committee and work out some reasonable plan for continuing a good collection of major works in that field. In time, as departmental interests shift, the library will have on hand the backbone of an adequate collection. Certain subjects do, of course, become obsolete and cease to be of further interest. But if, for example, a chemistry deparment should de-emphasize inorganic chemistry and concentrate on organic chemistry, an alert chemistry librarian should see that proper major items are still acquired in inorganic topics, since that subject is so vital a part of the literature of chemistry.

Sizes of Typical Research Collections—There are no workable formulas for determining the precise minimum size of a research collection in a sci-tech library for a given major discipline. Much depends upon local factors, such as the availability of related materials in other units of the library system or in other local institutions, the degree of cooperation between different units and institutions, and the size of the departments involved. A certain minimum is required, no matter what the size of the department, but the larger a department is the more divergent the research and the greater the demands upon the library.

Collection Development Policies

Role and Importance of Policies—It should be clear that the optimum size and content of a collection for a subject depend upon the instructional and research activities of the university. It should also be clear that a library cannot simply drift along, repeating past practices and merely hoping to be doing a proper job of building a suitable collection. A definite plan is needed, one which is regularly updated. Both the plan and the updating should be done in consultation with appropriate faculty members and research staff members. This has always been the situation in universities, yet it is even more important in these days of tighter university budgets for literature and the steadily rising costs of materials.

Different units of a library system should stay in close touch to eliminate as much duplication as possible. For example, it would be hard to justify having both a chemistry library and a life sciences, or biology, library developing equally strong collections in biochemistry. Or, in the case of nonscience departments, duplication of materials on industrial productivity in a library serving the industrial engineering department and one serving a business school would be equally wasteful of funds.

Extreme geographic distances between library units is one reason for allowing a certain amount of duplication to continue, but even then a given topic can sometimes be split between two libraries with a minimum of duplication.

Once faculty and research staff views are known, the librarian has to make the final decisions in areas where the faculty recommendations are not realistic, notifying them of the reasons for changes. Major changes have to be renegotiated, but minor ones need not be. Having the ability to make wise decisions regarding collections is one mark of a skilled professional sci-tech librarian.

Ideally, budgets should be drawn up after the goals for a collection are set. More frequently than not, however, librarians are given a set amount based upon previous years of experience rather than a more logical basis.

One of the few attempts to arrive at a more logical basis for collection size involves the Clapp-Jordan formula, which was described in an article written in 1965.[1] It attempts to specify ideal collection sizes in terms of the number of students, the number of Ph.D. programs, and other factors. Others have studied this plan and at least one article has been written in which a refinement of their formula is proposed. The author, McInnis, admits it is not an easy matter to derive a workable formula.[2]

Collection Development Policy Statements—In view of the importance of having policies for building a collection, it would be expected that university libraries would have such policies clearly written, in a usable form. However, this is not generally the case. More likely than not libraries do not have *any* written policy statements for building their collections. If they do, the documents are usually not uniform in format and style, making coordination within a particular library system difficult, if not impossible. Likewise, most are written in prose form so that it is not easy to locate a particular topic, nor is updating of the document easy. This is unfortunate in view of the need of libraries to be able to adopt new policies quickly to keep up with new developments in the field and changing local requirements.

One method to overcome some of these difficulties was devised by Columbia University Libraries, where a computer-based plan was put into effect.[3] It consists of a one-character code to indicate the intended type of collection sought in a given library unit (research, minimal, exhaustive, etc.), as well as a one-character code to indicate the type of language coverage sought (primarily English, primarily Western European, etc.). For example, a 5F collection would be the coding used for a research level collection having a wide range of foreign-language material plus English-language items. These codes are applied to the pertinent classes in the Library of Congress classification system. It results in a machine-readable record of which libraries at that university are collecting what subjects and at what degree of concentration. Printouts can be either by LC classification number (arranged in class order) or by class descriptors (arranged alphabetically). One of the main advantages it offers is the ease of updating the records; another is the uniformity of records. A collection of one-paragraph prose descriptions of each library supplements the machine-readable portion, so that special features of each collection which may be difficult to describe with a coding (such as the existence of strong map holdings or technical report collections) can be emphasized. General use of a well-recognized system like the LC classification would facilitate the comparison of one university library collection with another in this system. This system makes it simpler to spot overlapping of collection effort as well as to note areas where gaps in the collection are not being taken care of, whether it is used in analyzing the activities within one library system or within several systems.

Figure 2 shows a sample printout of one portion of the classified list prepared for Columbia Libraries. Spinoffs of the listing for all libraries can be made for any single library or group of library units. The original plan called for annual updating, with staff and faculty members contributing to the process of review of collection needs.

Stanford University Libraries have recently prepared a prose-type description of collection goals. Their method does not, however, solve the problems of updating, comparison of activity between units, and location of specific topics.

No matter what method is used, any effort at creating a written record of collection policies is worthwhile, if only to spur the process of analyzing existing practices at a university and subsequently to stimulate new goals.

Selection of Materials

Many factors affect a decision to purchase or not to purchase an item for a collection, or to accept a gift or added copy for a collection. The purpose of this section is to describe briefly the major considerations that go into the selection of materials, particularly for a sci-tech library. Different libraries have different criteria, depending upon the subject matter or type of collection maintained since a rare books library, for example, would have entirely different criteria for its selections.

In many universities the librarians in charge of subject units (such as chemistry, physics, and geology,) or their professional staff members do most of the selecting of new materials, getting a minimum of help from faculty members and other users. On the other hand, in some departments the faculty members make recommendations for new additions, thus aiding a librarian who is unsure of his judgment or in need of a second opinion. Still another method is to use staff members known as bibliographers for selection, utilizing those with appropriate subject backgrounds and not necessarily having library degrees.

Monographs

Subject Matter—This is obviously the most important factor in making a selection. The best book ever written on a subject is of no consequence to a library if it doesn't match the subject interest of that library. Usually the problem is not this simple, it being a question of how many books on the subject are already on hand, whether the one in question adds much to what is on hand, etc.

Level of Treatment—Whether a work is written for an undergraduate text, or for advanced scholars, or somewhere in between is extremely important. Most sci-tech libraries avoid purchasing undergraduate-level

```
L.C. CLASS        DESCRIPTOR

Q125-127          Science (History)
                     GLX  2W
                     SCI  4F

Q141-Q149         Science (Biography)
                     SCI  4F

Q175              Science (Philosophy)
                     SCI  3F [Formerly 4F
                               until 1960]

Q300-Q380         Cybernetics
                     BUS  1E
                     ENG  4F
                     MED  2E
                     PSY  2F
                     SCI  1E

QA                Mathematics (See classed
                     listing below)

QA3-QA7           Mathematics (Collected
                     works)
                     MAT  2F

QA47-QA59         Mathematics (Tables)
                     MAT  3E [Formerly 4F
                               until 1960]

QA76              Computer Science
                     BUS  3E
                     CHE  1E
                     ENG  4F [Engng. aspects]
                     MED  2E
                     PSY  2F
                     SIS  3F [Library
                               applications]
```

Figure 2   Collection development policy printout

textbooks. Yet, if there are no advance graduate courses or if no basic research is taking place, the library has little need for the most complex books on a subject.

Authorship and/or Sponsorship—A few well-known authors have such a good reputation in sci-tech subjects that a library can almost count on their monographs being well worth purchasing, sight unseen. Likewise, many technical and scientific societies sponsor works of such value that the selection of their publications is more or less required. Unfortunately, only a handful of books out of the total published has distinguished enough authorship or sponsorship to make this criterion widely usable for selection purposes.

Publisher—Experience will teach sci-tech librarians which publishers consistently produce high quality works, which ones have poor records, and which ones have spotty records. Some publishers publish mostly advanced works, while others specialize in undergraduate texts. All these bits of information aid the experienced person in selecting monographs. It should be noted that some publishers persist in reprinting older works but give them new introductions by some notable person, with the advertising subsequently giving the impression that it is an all-new work. Needless to say, librarians shun such publishers.

Quality of Production—Aside from the content and level of a work, such factors as quality of paper and binding or attractiveness of print style used can add a great deal to the value of a monograph. In some disciplines, such as the life sciences, the illustrations and plates are extremely important, so that the quality of such features should be carefully checked when appropriate. This implies that the monographs can be inspected before final decisions are made, which is not always possible.

Language in Which Written—As previously indicated, most sci-tech libraries choose only the very best monographs in foreign languages, and these usually are written in Western European tongues. The main reason is that few faculty-research staff users in the United States have enough facility with foreign languages to make such purchases worthwhile. In some disciplines the best works frequently are written in English, the most popular language of science and engineering, which is another reason for concentrating on English-language texts.

Costs—In view of the usually tight budgets for monographs in most university libraries, costs are very definitely a factor. A few works are so important they must be added regardless of cost, but borderline works are sometimes rejected because they seem overpriced for what they add to a collection. Once again, some publishers consistently charge more for a given size of work than other companies do, and alert librarians are not slow to notice this.

Sci-tech books are generally higher priced than those of other disciplines, as revealed in annual surveys appearing in *Publishers Weekly*. The 1974 version showed that the average science book in 1973 cost $17.34, versus an average of $12.20 for *all* types of books.[4] Technology books were also high, costing $15.38. No doubt, 1974 averages for science books of the type needed for advanced research could cost around $20 apiece, based on recent informal surveys of list prices for such works.

Age—This criterion is listed last because it is assumed that this section applies primarily to selecting current books, in which case age is not a factor. If retrospective literature selections are being made, then it is important to note that sci-tech books become less useful much sooner than those in nontechnical fields, with engineering books becoming obsolete more quickly than pure science books. Mathematics books have the longest useful life compared to other sciences and engineering.

One cannot realistically assign weights to these criteria, and the order in which they are listed is not necessarily the order of importance in all cases. The overall effect of consideration of the criteria makes up the process of effective selection.

Serials

Subject Matter—As in the case of monographs, subject matter is probably the primary factor in deciding upon subscribing to a periodical or other serial. No matter how great the quality or how modest the price, the subject must fit local needs.

Level of Treatment—This topic is also of prime importance in making a decision. A university chemistry library would have little use for a journal dealing with the prices of chemicals on a commercial scale. A physics department, where basic research is the prime faculty activity outside of the classroom, and where the doctorate is given, would have little interest in a journal concentrating on engineering applications of nuclear energy to power generation, whereas a journal centered on theoretical studies of nuclear physics would have a very definite place in the collection.

Sponsorship—Serials published by recognized scientific and engineering societies in the sci-tech world generally rate high with users. Many of these titles are indispensable to libraries serving the appropriate subject areas. As previously mentioned, some societies publish only one or two journals, while others publish a dozen or more. In many cases all of them are required for a first-rate collection. This is not to say that many fine journals are not published by commercial firms.

Quality of Production—Journals seem to be of more uniform quality than monographs, at least as far as English-language and Western European-language publications are concerned. However, the quality of the paper is not outstanding in many Soviet bloc and Latin-American titles. Some titles are needed in spite of their less-than-perfect quality of production.

Indexing—The inclusion or exclusion of a given periodical from the ranks of those regularly covered by periodical indexing and abstracting services is one more factor by which to judge its worth. Normally the better journals are all indexed, although it is not possible to predict what will happen to a very new title. But a good journal will soon be covered by one or more indexing services.

Language in Which Published—Journals in foreign languages are, in general, more apt to be required in any type of sci-tech collection than are foreign monographs. This is more important, of course, in the case of research than instructional collections. Western European-language journals are more commonly held in sci-tech libraries than those from Eastern European countries and other non-Roman alphabet publishers. There are exceptions, but this rule generally holds. Translations, on a cover-to-cover basis, are available for many important titles, which lessens the need for the original unless the information is urgently needed. The original is usually available several months (on the average) before the translation appears.

Costs—Rising costs of periodicals, an understandable process in view of rising prices for materials and labor, are causing the cancellation of titles, often of duplicate copies and sometimes of single subscriptions at a given sci-tech library. A recent survey showed that in 1973 prices for subscriptions to science periodicals increased from 12 to 17 percent on the average over 1972 averages, with journals in the fields of chemistry and physics averaging $65.47 per title, as contrasted with the average for all disciplines of $17.71.[5] All science journals averaged well above this latter figure, although the engineering cost ($24.38) was lower than that of the pure sciences. So sci-tech budgets are clearly under more strain in regard to periodical costs than those of other disciplines. Many titles are indispensable, however. Often all a library can do as prices rise is to stretch existing budgets by canceling lesser titles, or to obtain larger budgets, which has not been easy to accomplish in recent years.

No doubt other criteria could be added to the above, but these at least constitute the major factors in selection.

Weeding of Collections

Except for the few science-technology libraries that maintain collections of little-used, outdated materials for historical and archival reasons, most sci-tech units at universities must weed their collections according to some systematic, judicious plan. If the weeding is not done carefully and wisely, irreparable harm can be done to a collection. Consequently, many libraries are reluctant to even undertake it, preferring to seek more and more storage space as libraries become full. Another factor inhibiting weeding is the time it takes, involving knowledgeable librarians for long periods of time. Still another factor, to be discussed in more detail later in the chapter, is that of the growth of interlibrary networks and consortia, with reduction of overlapping of materials a major goal in many cases. This has stimulated interest in weeding.

As might be expected, the amount of material that should be weeded and discarded or offered to other libraries varies greatly from library to library. For example, if one library had a poor collection, including much worthless material, old elementary textbooks, or materials in bad physical condition, it would weed a higher percentage of material than would the library with a fine collection of material, and a minimum of out-of-scope items and of badly damaged copies.

Monographs

Age—In the areas of science and engineering, the most relentless enemy of the value of a work is age, due to the rapid strides with which scientific and technical advancements are made. However, as previously mentioned, age is of less importance in some disciplines. For example, certain geology works, particularly descriptions of local geological formations in various regions, are of long-range value. Changing interests of a library, a function of age, also play an important role in weeding. Another factor is the level of treatment. The date of last use of a monograph can help determine whether it should be weeded, if records such as date due slips are available to ascertain the time and frequency of use. (Note that this section does not apply to classic works, a few of which are hundreds of years old.)

Level of Treatment—There are outstanding works in each discipline which should never be weeded because they are still very valuable to workers in the field. Usually these are written on an advanced rather than elementary level. Any weeding effort that includes such works would be most upsetting to knowledgeable users of the library.

In general, the more fundamental and theoretical the treatment of a subject, the less need there is for weeding, since basic principles show their age less than detailed descriptions of equipment or particular applications. Textbooks for undergraduates also age quickly; libraries are well advised to avoid collecting them as much as possible. For example, a monograph discussing the phenomenon of radio wave transmission, written on a highly mathematical level, would have much longer value in a collection than a work describing particular designs of radio transmitters. Both books have their value, but the latter soon becomes outdated and of historical interest only. Most mathematics books (aside from those emphasizing applications) have a long life relative to monographs in other sci-tech disciplines.

Authorship—Closely related to the question of quality is that of authorship. Works by outstanding scientists and engineers should be retained indefinitely—if the subjects are still in scope—because they are major titles and may still be in relatively frequent use. No doubt the records on the amount of use of a monograph, if available, give some clue as to which authors are important. If the person doing the weeding is not sure, then a more knowledgeable person should double check the candidate titles for weeding.

Another criterion to keep in mind at any university is that works written by a person connected with that university, such as a faculty member or even a former faculty member, should be retained more or less regardless of their value, since they constitute a record of the scholarship and instructional activity at that university. Checking the title page of a work usually discloses the affiliation of the author(s), at least at the time of writing.

Language in Which Written—In most American university sci-tech libraries, a monograph written in a foreign language has to have unusual value to warrant its indefinite retention. The users' lack of language skills is the main reason for this situation. Some works are useful in spite of the language in which they are written because of graphs, equations, and the like which can be used without a knowledge of the text, but this is not always the case. Foreign classics are not easily recognized in this country, so again, a competent person should check weeded titles.

Physical Condition—Other things being equal, a monograph in bad physical condition (e.g., brittle paper, torn binding, mutilated text) has less value to a collection than one in good shape. On the other hand, the monumental works in a field need to be kept regardless of condition and should be repaired, if possible. If not, a replacement copy or a microform version should be obtained.

Serials

Because serials usually have a distinct set of characteristics—holding good for many years and covering many volumes—they can be evaluated much more quickly per volume than an equal number of monographs. Whatever the rating one gives a periodical it usually applies to all its volumes, so that no one would be likely, for example, to keep volumes 5, 10, and 24 of a run of bound volumes and reject the rest. This might happen in a monographic series, where the subject matter of some volumes is no longer of interest, but would not apply to periodicals. However, this does not preclude the establishment of cutoff dates so that the most recent fifteen years of a periodical, for example, are retained and the others discarded. Reliance is then placed on other sources for the older material.

Basic weeding considerations are given below.

Age—The effect of age depends, as in the case of monographs, upon several factors, one of which is subject matter. The best journal ever published on the subject of the design of steam locomotives will have little value to most libraries now except for historical purposes, and one set in a regional depository might suffice. On the other hand, all volumes of the *Journal of the American Chemical Society,* probably the chief journal of the society, should be on all university campuses, even if some of the older volumes have to be placed in an accessible storage area because of space problems. The value of the material to the faculty and research staff makes all the difference, in spite of age. For journals that fall between these two extremes, age has a place in determining which volumes are needed on campus and which can be weeded. The more basic the subject matter, the more long-lasting the value, as was noted with monographs. Certain disciplines, such as mathematics and basic research in the sciences, are less affected by age than those involving production techniques, equipment, and the like. And as in the case of monographs, changing interests of the university may make once-valuable journals literally useless now and in the future. If, for example, courses in ocean engineering are no longer offered, it would be rather pointless to keep volumes if the subject matter no longer has any bearing.

Level and Quality of Treatment—Similar to the case of monographs, the type of treatment of a subject affects the value of serials. For example, a periodical that consists almost entirely of news items, ephemera of a particular trade or industry, or statistics available elsewhere has very little value to the average sci-tech library after ten years or so, and could be safely weeded, providing a set were available in a regional source. Yet a journal devoted to basic research findings would probably have to be retained indefinitely, as long as the subject matter was related to current research and instructional programs. (For the points related to this subject, namely the relationship of basic research journals to a longer useful life than those devoted to techniques and hardware, see the preceding section on age.)

Sponsorship—Publications of societies, institutes, and the like tend, on the average, to be more valuable over a long period than those without a professional sponsorship. The wealth of talent available for supervision and contributions, an unbiased approach to controversial issues, and other intellectual factors favor such a sponsorship. Of course, many commercially published journals are excellent and are valuable to a collection.

Language in Which Written—Sci-tech collections have a much greater need for back issues of foreign-language periodicals than for monographs in such languages, as long as these titles meet all the requirements set forth here. The coverage of such titles by major indexing services is one reason they continue to be valuable, and the greater specificity of periodical articles as compared to monographs also adds value. However, the three most likely languages to warrant retention in most sci-tech disciplines are still French, German, and Russian. Other languages, of course, are involved in major periodicals, but these three are by far the most familiar languages. Fortunately, many of the major

Soviet journals are available in English translations, as are some major Japanese works, but the total number of translations is still not large, and prices continue to be rather high compared to the original editions. Translated editions do, however, represent a good value because of their time savings for interested readers and because of their lower cost than individual translations.

In a few disciplines some foreign-language journals in Oriental or even more esoteric languages may be so important that it would be necessary to keep such issues beyond the first five years or so, when they are relatively current. Periodicals on fisheries, for example, include many major titles issued in Japanese, so that a blanket rule about the value of older Oriental titles would not apply here.

Physical Condition—The quality of the paper and binding of serials must be considered. If the level of either is too low, then alternatives to storage, if that is called for, must be found. Many major titles are available on microfilm, which is the usual choice selected if the original is not worth saving. But for a borderline title, the question of the physical condition may help decide the question about weeding.

Most microfilmed journals are on 16 mm film, although a few are on 35 mm. The space savings are considerable, aside from the question of cost of purchasing the microfilm.

Storage Collections

One useful alternative to weeding and removal of literature is to establish a storage area for little-used materials. The area should be shelved by size, have narrower aisles than public shelving, and be within a few minutes' walk from the library, with pages going as required, at least once per day, if necessary.

One useful method in selecting materials for storage is to base selection primarily on the date of last use of a volume; the method is explained in the article by Trueswell.[6] Essentially, one checks the circulation records of material currently on loan and determines the date of last use (prior to the current loan) for all items if such data can be determined. Then the materials are grouped so that it can be determined what percentage of items circulating were last borrowed six months before, one year before, and so forth. When one has determined the length of time of previous loans which includes say 97 percent of the material currently on loan, items which have not been borrowed in that time period are very unlikely to be requested again. (In this case the chances would be 97 to 3.) One could select any figure and make the storage selection on that basis, but at least 95 percent is recommended to reduce requests for items in storage to a low number. This system works best when book cards or due date slips are used, so that previous loans can be ascertained easily. This is not the case with transaction slips or computer records, where normally only the current loan is recorded.

A careful analysis of the factors affecting selection of works for storage is found in the book by Fussler.[7] He describes the differences between disciplines, including the sciences, in regard to suitability for storage, and notes that age was an important factor in choosing science books.

Cooperative Agreements

Cooperative agreements as to collection policies have existed between different library systems for many decades. A major library in one city, for example, might reach an agreement with another local library of some status as to which of the two will continue collecting materials in several disciplines. The success of such agreements has varied, depending upon the degree of formality involved, the personal feelings of library administrators inheriting such arrangements from their predecessors, changing needs of the libraries involved, and other reasons.

Now there seems to be a resurgence of interest in such plans, involving in some cases many libraries in several states. The Center for Research Libraries (CRL) in Chicago, which originally planned to serve only libraries in the Midwest, has since expanded to include libraries from all parts of the United States. In 1973 talks began among the administrators of the libraries of three universities (Harvard, Columbia, and Yale) and the New York Public Library in the interest of establishing a consortium of the four units, particularly in regard to cooperative agreements for collections. Since then, discussions and funding have reached the point where the formation of the Research Libraries Group (RLG), as it is named, is no longer in question. Just as CRL enables its members to reduce somewhat the number of periodical titles actively subscribed to, so will RLG affect its members' policies. In addition to serials, selection of expensive monographic works will likely be affected, as will be storage requirements for older materials.

Thus, it is obvious that any collection development policy established at an institution newly involved in a cooperative plan will have to be reevaluated in terms of the new agreements. New groupings might be established, such as having one library responsible for collecting all Oriental series in science, or another to collect all translations of Soviet sci-tech periodicals. Both selection and weeding would be affected by these agreements. The possible number of combinations is large, and time will tell which type of plan is the most successful.

Budgets

With tighter budgets all types of libraries—public, academic, school, and special—are working under considerable pressure to keep expenditures down for their operations, including collections and binding. Inflation in book and serial prices, as well as lower purchasing power of the dollar abroad, have meant that any library that does not receive a larger budget each year for collections and binding is actually going backwards rather than standing still.

There is no exact formula as to what is a proper amount to spend for collections and binding, but some statistics may give the reader an idea of the current situation. A study made by the Association of Research Libraries, which was restricted to six large privately supported universities in the United States, shows that the average portion of their total budgets spent for collections for the period 1968-1973 has varied from a low of 22.5 percent to a high of 28.0 percent, while binding costs varied from a low of 2.5 percent to a high of 3.9 percent.[8] In terms of dollars, the average cost of collections ranged from $1.4 million to $1.65 million, while binding was in the range of $175,000 to $231,000.

In terms of the amount allocated for sci-tech libraries, at one large university the amounts for the fiscal year 1973/1974 were as follows:

Monographs	$ 41,400 (18%)
Serials	138,000 (60%)
Continuations	27,000 (12%)
Binding	23,000 (10%)

These sums were to be divided among the half dozen or more units serving science and technology. The total collection of the units was around 350,000 volumes, and around 4,000 serials were received currently.

The preparation of the total budget for a university library system is a long, complex procedure, involving the director and many others. The head of each library unit should be asked to submit recommendations for budgets, even though financial limitations may make the amounts requested impossible to meet. Nevertheless, the budget process should allow for this participation.

Once the total library budget is allocated, in some systems the one in charge of the sci-tech libraries, such as a division head, is given a lump sum and asked to make recommendations as to the actual final allocation for each sci-tech unit, if there is more than one. There are many reasons for allocating serial funds first, as well as continuation funds, since subscriptions and orders for multipart works need first priority. This means that funds for monographs and binding get allocated last, giving them a lower priority than the other portions of the budget. While the practice is understandable, in view of the importance of serials to sci-tech libraries, it has meant that monograph collections have tended to suffer in order to keep serial collections as near normal as possible.

Until or unless funds for collections become more available, librarians will have to continue to pore over their operations and collection policies in search of ways to reduce costs.

Selection Tools

There are many sources available for getting information about new serials and monographs, both new and old.

Publishers' Advertisements—These can be a very valuable means for keeping abreast of new titles, both for serials and for monographs. One has to learn to take claims of certain publishers with the proverbial grain of salt, both as to the worth of a publication or even its existence. It is not unknown for a few publishers to advertise a work that has not even been written in final form, and if response is too low the work is never published. In the meanwhile some libraries may have put aside funds for the publication, only to eventually lose those funds if the work is not issued in a reasonable time (since many universities do not allow mortgaged funds from one year to be used for another purpose in succeeding years). However, the majority of publishers are very ethical, and their advertising pieces are truthful. One problem is that of being on more than one mailing list, but duplicate brochures are easily spotted and discarded. Publishers' annual catalogs are well worth filing for later use.

National Bibliographies—All librarians are readily familiar with standard tools for identifying current monographs, such as *Books in Print* and *Cumulative Book Index.* A recent index is *Sci-Tech Books in Print,* which is limited to books in the categories of science and engineering. As for serials, the most well-known index is *Ulrich's International Periodicals Index.* Besides the listings of all types of monographs found in *Weekly Record* (formerly a part of *Publishers Weekly*) and *Book Publishing Record,* there is great use made in sci-tech circles of *Technical Book Review Index* and *New Technical Books* (New York Public Library). The latter two have the advantage of including annotations. (More details regarding these titles can be found in Chapter 10.)

Book Reviews—Another excellent source of information on new books is that of the book review sections found in many periodicals. Some are much more useful than others, and some are much more promptly issued after the monographs are published than others. But frequently the reviews are written by experts and thus one benefits from their evaluations.

Exhibits—Most library conferences of any size and those of information science, engineering, and scientific societies include booths for publishers, which provides a good way to keep informed of new publications. Occasionally, one finds combined exhibits, which makes browsing even quicker.

Approval plans—Some book wholesalers in this country and abroad allow libraries to set up approval plans whereby books selected by the wholesalers to match the established interest profiles of the libraries are sent on approval. This allows library selection officers to see a work before making a final selection, which is a great aid in making good choices, since an announcement slip or an item in a bibliography is no substitute for actually seeing a work. The growing literature on this subject includes an annotated literature survey on the costs and value of the process prepared by McCullough[9] and a moderately critical article by Dobbyn.[10]

Book Stores—Although many librarians do not have easy access to good book stores for sci-tech books, those in this position can benefit from the browsing possible among the titles.

Notes

[1]Verner W. Clapp and Robert T. Jordan, "Quantitative Criteria for Adequacy of Academic Library Collections," *College & Research Libraries* 26, no. 5 (September 1965): 371-380.
[2]R. Marvin McInnis, "The Formula Approach to Library Size: An Empirical Study of Its Efficacy in Evaluating Research Libraries," *College & Research Libraries* 30, no. 3 (May 1972): 190-198.
[3]J. Yavarkovsky, E. Mount, and H. Kordish, "Computer-based Collection Development Statements for a University Library," *ASIS Proceedings* 10 (1973): 240-241.
[4]"1973: U.S. Book Industry Statistics: Titles, Prices, Sales Trends," *Publishers Weekly* 205, no. 5 (February 4, 1974): 53, 56-58.
[5]Norman B. Brown, "Price Indexes for 1974," *Library Journal* 99, no. 13, (July 1974): 1775-1779.
[6]Richard W. Trueswell, "A Quantitative Measure of User Circulation Requirements and Its Possible Effect on Stack Thinning and Multiple Copy Determination." *American Documentation* 16, no. 1 (January 1965): 20-25.
[7]Herman H. Fussler, *Patterns in the Use of Books in Large Research Libraries* (Chicago: University of Chicago Press, 1961), 283 p.
[8]Association of Research Libraries, *Academic Library Statistics: 1963/64-1971/72* (Washington D.C., 1972), 119 p. (ED 082 791).
[9]Kathleen McCullough, "Approval Plans: Vendor Responsibility and Library Research: A Literature Survey and Discussion," *College & Research Libraries* 33, no. 5 (September 1972): 368-381.
[10]Margaret Dobbyn, "Approval Plan Purchasing in Perspective," *College & Research Libraries* 33, no. 6 (November 1972): 480-484.

6

Technical Services

The term *technical services* is used here in the traditional sense, that is,
referring to the processes concerned with the acquisition, cataloging or
indexing, bibliographic control, and preservation of items in the library
collection. It can apply both to printed and nonprinted materials. As will
be seen, many of these processes are rarely carried out in science-
technology libraries or by personnel assigned to such libraries. However,
sci-tech libraries are highly dependent upon the skillful, efficient operation of such processes by other units in order to provide adequate service
to their users. Sci-tech personnel participate in a few technical services,
either by themselves or in cooperation with other units of the library
system.

Readers desiring a thorough, detailed description of technical services
written at the student's level are referred to the text by Tauber.[1] It is useful
even though it needs updating.

Centralized Technical Services

Most university library systems now have centralized technical
services. This means that most cataloging, book and serial ordering,
budgetary recordkeeping for expenditures, binding supervision, and
local binding processes, as well as catalog card or book catalog prepara-

tion, are done in one central location for the library system. These units are usually located in a large central building housing the main library. Those universities whose library is confined to one building are obviously centralized, but those systems that have many separate units scattered over a campus have had to choose whether or not to centralize these operations. As indicated above, most of them have done so. The savings in manpower as well as the need for overall coordination of effort point towards the advantages of a centralized system. The librarians in sci-tech units, for example, thus would rely on the central technical service groups to place orders, do the necessary cataloging and bibliographic control tasks, send out binding or do local binding, and keep the financial records of these transactions.

Cataloging—In large systems there may be several catalogers who do nothing but sci-tech monograph and serials cataloging. They become well acquainted with the sci-tech librarians' collections and needs, often having some collegiate background in these subjects. Some catalogers make trips, as needed, to individual units to check certain points not clear at the main library. Depending upon the style and personalities of the librarians involved, it is possible to have very good working conditions under a system such as described. It should be noted that the advent of the Library of Congress MARC tapes is reducing the amount of original cataloging universities must do now.

Catalog card preparation and revisions, establishment of filing rules—all these and similar processes are carried on in the main cataloging department. Each library unit has its own card catalog, or, in the case of more modern systems, its own book catalog. (In time each library may have its entire catalog on-line, although the costs of doing this for large collections are, at this time, prohibitive.) Keeping the catalog filed with all new cards received from the central unit is normally the task of each unit's staff, although some libraries have at least given thought to, if not adopted, the plan of having mobile units of card filers who move to where the catalogs are, working out of the central catalog department.

One library system—that at Georgia Tech—has placed its entire catalog on a set of microfiches, with sets maintained at various places around the campus, including departmental offices. They are able to use COM (computer-output-microfilm) processes for making and updating the set. Other libraries have been converting to book catalogs, printed by computers. Early work on this was done at one of the Stanford University libraries. In the last few years one of the country's largest libraries—the

New York Public Library—has stopped producing catalog cards for items acquired since then, and now relies entirely on a multivolume book catalog. Many book catalogs cumulate each quarter, then once each year, so that only one current issue and the previous annual issues need be consulted. Larger cumulations become quite expensive to produce.

A project which has caught the eye of the library world is that of the Ohio College Library Center (OCLC), where cooperative services are offered to member institutions around the country. One service is that of an on-line shared cataloging system, enabling members to query the holdings via cathode ray tube terminals connected by telephone to the OCLC computer. If, for example, a query shows a given title to be in the system, a catalog card can be ordered at that time via the phone link, with delivery made to the member library within seven days.[2] Catalog data supplied by OCLC cost less than buying printed cards. A review of the project by Kilgour noted that in its first year (it became operational in August 1971) over half a million cards were produced in the off-line card production branch of the Center.[3] There were three hundred libraries in twenty-two states and the District of Columbia using the on-line system for book cataloging by the end of its third year, when it cataloged its millionth volume. Seven thousand books are cataloged daily, with over 50 percent of the system records being supplied by participating libraries.[4]

These developments show that cataloging is by no means a static, unchanging process, thanks to the applications made possible by the computer and microforms. It is difficult to predict what innovations may appear in the years ahead.

Acquisitions—The selection of vendors, the placing of orders for monographs and serials, and the keeping of financial and bibliographic records of these transactions traditionally belong to a central acquisitions department at most libraries. The need for a central record of what is on order, of standardized purchasing forms and bill payments, or specialized knowledge of suitable vendors for different types of materials—these are some of the reasons why a centralized acquisition plan is so commonly used.

Acquisitions functions, like those of cataloging, are also being modernized, using the dual aids of computers and microforms. One of the most common uses of computers in this work is for preparing orders, in which a machine-readable record is captured as a byproduct of the task. From this record a computer-printed listing of materials currently on order can be prepared, checks can be prepared for university purchasing departments (or whomever else is involved in writing checks to pay the library's bills), and a record kept of the progress of the incoming monographs through the technical services area to the ordering library. Many libraries now have such a computer printout, which each week shows the status of each monograph in process; other libraries use a COM (computer-output-microfilm) process and can produce the record on microfiche. This change was made recently at Columbia University partly because of the rising costs of paper; now only ten to fifteen fiche need to be produced per week. Sets are distributed to a few key points in the library system, at much lower cost than the printed records formerly used.

The computerization of serial records is one area in which effort could be spent profitably. Since most universities subscribe to tens of thousands of periodicals and other serials, to put them into machine-readable form is a sizable task. From this record can be produced union lists of serials, which can also be arranged by subjects, library units, or other variations. Keeping track of which invoices have been paid and which are still unpaid is a very vexing problem, leading to uncertainty as to what portion of the serials budget should be reserved for unpaid invoices and how much remains for new serials. Computerization is the obvious solution, in spite of the difficulties of establishing a viable program for this complicated area.

A few libraries have experimented with computerized serial check-in records rather than using the familiar manual system. However, there are many problems in making this workable in a large university system.

An overall view of the problems of computerizing technical service processes is given in an article by Veaner.[5] The University of Minnesota's Biomedical Library is experimenting with mini-computers for the use of one university library unit, including its technical service operations, with the possibility of expanding it to university-wide applications. That university has already put its thousands of serials titles in machine-readable form, a project carried on prior to the mini-computer project. Having a computer reserved exclusively for a library system may be worth investigating in some universities, but careful thought and planning would obviously have to be done to determine the feasibility and wisdom of such a step. In most universities the library is allotted time on the university computer(s).

Conversion of acquisition records to an on-line basis is feasible for certain sizes of operations, but for large-scale use the costs would be hard to justify. It has not been done at any of the largest university libraries to date.

As in the case of centralized cataloging, the sci-tech units can manage very well with centralized acquisitions. They can suggest to acquisition staff members special sources for difficult items to locate, make recommendations as to problems arising with serials vendors, etc. With the proper cooperative attitudes, the system can function very well for all concerned.

Binding and Preservation—Most universities have one center for keeping records of binding invoices, for selection of binders, and for establishing procedures and specifications for the process, as well as for doing certain simplified binding on the premises (usually for pamphlets, certain paperback books, and the like).

Sci-tech libraries usually have less need for pamphlet binding than libraries in the social sciences or humanities, where the large quantity of paperback books on reserve is given this treatment in order to protect them. On the other hand, sci-tech units have many more serials to bind than the other above-named disciplines.

No matter how speedily the journals are bound and returned, there are always requests for journals that are at the bindery. To reduce this to the absolute minimum, a few general principles have been found helpful.

One rule is to try to send the most-used journals during an intersession period, or at least during the summer months, if that part of the year is less active than others. This would include the binding of major periodical indexes, such as *Chemical Abstracts* for a chemistry library. A second rule is to coordinate the date of binding with other libraries in the system which subscribe to the same journal, so that the unforgiveable sin of binding—having *two* sets of the same journal at the bindery at the same time—is avoided. A third rule is to reexamine the needs of the library periodically to see if it is necessary to bind each title currently being bound. For example, some journals would be nearly as useful and would take up much less room if the library kept only a few recent years and purchased the microfilm version for long-term retention. Obviously this is not feasible for heavily used titles, but even these might be acceptable on microfilm for the volumes which were fifteen to twenty years old or older, keeping only the newer years in full size. The journals that lend themselves best to microfilm retention versions are the news-items types, the second- and third-rate journals, or the older volumes of first-rate journals. With many titles now commercially available on microfilm, it is seldom necessary for a library to film its own issues. There are differences of opinion about the value of microfilm reels or cartridges, the latter needing no threading in a machine of the type designed for cartridges. For large collections the extra cost of cartridges may not be worth the money.

Another somewhat obvious alternative to rule three, if the amount of use is low enough, is to decide that the library would not need either binding or microfilm copies, and that merely discarding (through library channels) older issues according to the retention schedule set up for each title would be sufficient.

Besides deciding what titles are to be bound, it is traditionally the responsibility of each sci-tech unit to gather its issues, order missing issues, prepare the prescribed binding records for each volume, then send completed sets of issues to the central binding office, usually in the main library building. The issues are sent from there to the bindery, then returned to the central binding office for checking against invoices, and finally are usually sent to the shelflister in the main library prior to return to the originating library. A charge-out to the bindery in the circulation record of the originating library, which is a necessary step in handling requests for these volumes, can then be discarded and the volumes added to the local shelflist.

In some subject areas, such as geology, there are many volumes that require a pocket for maps inside the back cover. This normally calls for an extra charge, or may preclude having the volume bound at what is called by various names, such as "economy binding" or "low-cost binding," indicating a general class in which certain choices are no longer possible. This means that usually only one color of the library system's choice is used for all titles, extra charges are levied for more than a few lines of spine labeling, extra features (such as the pockets mentioned above) are not available, no collating or advertisement removal is done, and a definite limit on thickness is imposed (around 2 1/2 inches). If libraries experiment with this type of binding and find it satisfactory for titles not likely to have extremely hard wear, then a means of stretching the binding budget has been found. Many libraries have been giving all journals the same type "A" binding regardless of whether their use warranted such expense. Tighter budgets have forced them to reexamine these practices.

Efforts to introduce some automation in getting journals from the unit libraries to the bindery and back have been undertaken by certain commercial binders. One plan features the automatic creation of binding slips by a computer, using data built into a record for each title as to the number of volumes per year and number of duplicate subscriptions on the campus. However, a lot of clerical work will still be necessary to complete these tasks.

A recent trend in research libraries, closely related to the binding and general care of books, is that of a more systematic effort to preserve badly damaged literature. It could range from simple repairs to expensive treatment of rare books. Lamination of leaves that are deteriorating is one such process. In order to give more attention to their deteriorating collections, several university libraries have recently appointed librarians to serve as preservation officers, with augmented budgets over the usual funds allotted for binding to make inroads on a very serious problem common to most research libraries.

Technical Service Financial Records—The central technical service units are usually responsible for preparing the records showing details of expenditures, allotments, encumbrances, and other features for literature and binding for each of the library units. These are now prepared by computers, appearing as monthly printouts. Figure 1 (Chapter 3) is an example of a computer-printed monthly statement for a unit at one university. Near the end of a budget year, semimonthly statements may become necessary in order to bring the year to a close with budgets as nearly exhausted (but not overspent) as possible. The central office sees that checks are prepared (if it does not issue them itself, with prior university approval for such a plan), keeps the official records of invoices paid, and works with vendors in making adjustments to invoices, where necessary.

Decentralized Technical Services

Very few sci-tech libraries at universities are involved in organizational arrangements whereby they have their own technical service units. One example is that of the engineering and physical science libraries at UCLA, where catalogers are assigned to those units, working in the engineering library. Closeness to the collections being cataloged and more awareness of the needs of users are some of the advantages of this arrangement.

It is more common for law libraries and medical libraries at universities to have their own technical service units, working within the units, than for sci-tech libraries. But here the personnel in the technical service groups still report organizationally to the appropriate heads of departments in the central technical service group, thus helping to maintain uniformity of procedures and standards with the central technical services unit.

Other Organizational Arrangements

Besides the two basic arrangements discussed so far, other methods of organizing the staff have been used at different universities. One variation has recently been established at Columbia University, where its rather traditional technical service division has been divided into two parts.[6] One part, known as the Resources Group, is concerned with the cataloging (both original and with LC copy) of materials, along with collection development and utilization of resources. Another part of the library is known as the Support Group, which includes responsibility for acquisitions, in-process data, budget statements, and card production. These two groups serve the main library and all the individual units of the library system, although the medical and law libraries have their own acquisition and cataloging staffs who report to these two groups.

As libraries undergo self-analysis or else commission surveys by outside consultants, other patterns of organization will appear on the scene. What works best for one university might not be best for another, hence the value of each institution's making use of what is best for itself.

Notes

[1] Maurice F. Tauber, *Technical Services in Libraries: Acquisitions, Cataloging, Classification, Binding, Photographic Reproduction and Circulation Operations* (New York: Columbia University Press, 1954), 487 p.

[2] "OCLC Cataloging Service: Savings Cited," *Library Journal* 99, no. 5 (March 1, 1974): 612.

[3] Frederick C. Kilgour and others, "The Shared Cataloging System of the Ohio College Library Center," *Journal of Library Automation* 5, no. 3 (September 1972): 157-183.

[4] "OCLC Claims Milestone: One Million Mark in Cataloging," *Library Journal* 99, no. 18 (October 15, 1974): 2567.

[5]Allen B. Veaner, "The Application of Computing to Library Technical Processing," *College & Research Libraries* 31, no. 1 (January 1970): 36-42.

[6]Booz, Allen and Hamilton, Inc., *Organization and Staffing of the Libraries of Columbia University: A Case Study* (Westport, Conn.: Redgrave Information Resources Corporation, 1973), 210 p.

7

Reader Services

A university library system could have an excellent collection, a well-organized set of indexes and retrieval tools for extracting information from the collection, attractive facilities, and a well-trained staff, and yet fail miserably. The missing ingredient is the library user. All of the above aspects of a library system are vital parts of a planned effort to aid the user, and the extent to which a library is serving the user is probably the ultimate test of its overall effectiveness. A library in which a collection is less than excellent but which has a strong service group giving active, imaginative support to the instructional and research needs of the members of the university community is performing more usefully than one with a better collection in which the user is given an indifferent type of service. Most libraries strive to be strong in all aspects—collections, facilities, and service, but service is, in the eyes of the user, the portion of the library he or she is most apt to remember the longest. For example, how many libraries with beautiful facilities manage to leave the user with an unpleasant memory because of a desk attendant who was impatient or a librarian who gave only perfunctory assistance? It is not a rare phenomenon, unfortunately.

Reader services, then, are a very important part of the activities making up a library system. They can range from the simple task of charging out books at a loan desk to the location of illusive information on complex topics. The way in which they are performed and advertised on the campus is as important as the variety of services themselves. As a matter of fact, one survey showed that faculty members at six universities and state colleges were, on the average, unaware of 50 percent of the reference services offered by the libraries at their schools.[1] This survey, based on a sample of over one thousand faculty members (of which 73 percent took part), questioned them about the simple library tools, bibliographic instruction in classes, or conducting literature searches. Clearly librarians must develop better techniques of advertising their wares if our patrons are to increase their usage of these services. Just performing the services for them is not enough. When faculty members or students do use these services, the library staff member must be pleasant, accurate, and energetic in the performance of the service if the users are to remember the experience in a positive manner.

One general rule, then, in selecting staff members for reader service units is to select those people most likely to give the style of service that makes users feel that the library really cares about their welfare. Unskilled pleasantness is not enough to enable one to perform detailed reference work successfully, but, on the other hand, skilled unpleasantness is worse for library relations. The happy medium is to find staff members who are not only tactful in their handling of users but also skilled in the techniques of the tasks involved in the work.

Circulation Systems

The time-honored goal of the library—to provide proper conditions for the maximum use of materials by its patrons—lies at the heart of circulation activities. This all-important function is the one most users think of in considering their relationship to a library. They may know vaguely that some staff members spend all their time cataloging books, selecting them, ordering them, or binding them. But the staff members most prominent to them are the ones manning the circulation areas. Thus, staffing in such positions is very important because of the potential good or harm such staff members can do for the library-user relationship. The supervisors of all units, including sci-tech libraries, need to convey the importance of good service by staff members working in circulation areas. Comments of users, personal observations, surveys—all have their place in keeping the supervisor aware of how users are treated at circulation desks. It is far better that the supervisor quickly spot below-average standards of service and correct them than receive complaints from users and then take action.

The rules governing the circulation of materials vary tremendously from one library system to another. Even from one library to another in the same university there are often differences. In the latter case the users may be perplexed as to why one science library loans journals for two weeks and another on the same campus might not allow them to circulate at all. Part of the reason may be habit—the users are accustomed to local rulings that may have been in effect for decades. Another is faculty opinions, based at least in part on the nature of their work. Chemists, for example, tend to be very active in laboratory work in which quick access to the literature during the course of a day (or night) is quite vital to their work; hence, they tend to favor a restriction on loans of journals. They want to be sure a given reference is in the library when they want it. On the other hand, professors in a discipline like geology, where laboratory work is centered on instructional purposes and where projects are generally on a long-term basis, tend to favor journal loans, except in the case of a few key journals which they might wish to count on finding in the library at all times. Thus local needs vary in different disciplines. Some libraries, particularly those which consolidate many subject libraries into one, are able to find common circulation rules that satisfy all disciplines, but it is not an easy task.

The circulation of journals has been eased by improved photocopying equipment. This helps those who need more time to study an article from a journal that is not allowed to circulate. Although the future course of federal legislation regarding photocopying is difficult to predict, many librarians feel that the "fair use" concept of allowing a patron to make one copy of an article or a portion of a monographic work in lieu of handcopying is apt to remain a feature of future regulations. If this does not happen, the habits of most library users at universities will change, particularly in regard to serials, in view of their great importance in sci-tech libraries.

Because of the difficulties of finding regulations that suit everyone, it should not be surprising that a survey of sci-tech library units which I conducted in 1972 showed that circulation rules and hours of service were the two most common areas for complaints, with each of these matters accounting for 18 percent of the total complaints, according to the librarians questioned.[2] Sci-tech libraries, like their sister units on the campuses, tend to give more generous loans to faculty members, with graduates less favored and undergraduates having even less privileges. The justification for this policy is that the needs of users vary according to their rank (faculty versus student, for example) and that, understandably, a faculty member might need a six-month loan of a monograph whereas students could manage with two weeks. Actually, many libraries allow two or three renewals, so that a book not in demand can be kept legally by a student for two or more months. One-semester loans for Ph.D. candidates are not uncommon. Most systems wisely require *all* users to return materials after two weeks if there are other requesters waiting.

A very detailed account of loan policies for faculty members is found in an article by Haviland, in which he describes a survey of eighty-four universities.[3] Interestingly, only three out of the total group allowed faculty members unrestricted loans of monographs; over half set a limit of one year. Bound periodicals generally were limited to one week or less. In view of the trend toward tighter controls on loans and the corresponding greater availability of photocopying equipment, it is safe to predict that a survey taken now would show shorter loan periods to faculty members than those given in this survey.

Materials on reserve generally are loaned for much shorter periods because the expected demand for them is high. Reserve loans during the hours the library is open may be for as short a time as two hours, sometimes restricted to the room; overnight and three days are other popular time intervals. The faculty members responsible for putting items on reserve generally recommend the proper loan periods for each, based on their knowledge of the expected use of the material. Extra copies are often available for removal before the library closing hour; this is a reasonable rule to follow.

Because of security problems with certain popular items which might be stolen, libraries sometimes put them on reserve, just to give them extra protection. These might be regular monographs, reference books, or even bound journals.

Many libraries at universities have automated their reserve records in order to reduce clerical workloads and to obtain, as a byproduct, special indexes needed by the library, such as one arranged by author or title and the other by name of the faculty member. Inventory data, useful to libraries with large stocks to keep track of for reserve uses, can also be included in such a system. Speed is vital in processing reserve lists since students and professors can be greatly inconvenienced if items are not on reserve in time. Computer systems have been found useful to reduce the time needed to get material on reserve, but it should be noted that professors who are tardy in returning lists can cause delays no computer system or efficient library staff can overcome in getting materials ready.

Fines for lost books or overdue books are not pleasant to have to impose, but most libraries have found no workable substitute for this system. Rules concerning circulation and fines should be posted prominently in libraries, and the fines should be applied fairly. One of the big problems in this area is to decide whether or not to accept the statements of users who are positive they returned books; sometimes they are quite right and sometimes they are not. One possible rule to follow is to accept such a claim the first time from a borrower, but to be very careful such a person does not get another fine waived unless it is a clear case of library error. As in all dealings with the public, it is imperative to treat all patrons courteously and fairly, no matter how provoking their conduct or remarks may be. Charges and processing costs for lost books are equally necessary, with payments usually handled by the bursar's office. At some schools unpaid library bills, until finally settled, will hold up students' registration and graduation.

Hours of Service

There are no hard and fast rules for determining the hours sci-tech libraries should be open. Much depends upon the number of libraries, the habits of users at that institution, the existence of keys for graduates and faculty members, and numerous other factors.

If there is only one library unit, the cost of keeping it open long hours is minimal compared to keeping several units open. Providing reference service from morning to mid-evening is also possible under such an arrangement. But to provide professional service beyond normal daytime hours for several sci-tech units is not inexpensive.

At some universities there are certain hours when almost no one requires a library and other hours when they are extremely well patronized. For example, Friday night at most universities is a low point of library use, and many do not bother to stay open after 5:00 or 6:00 P.M. On the other hand, Sunday afternoons and early evening are very popular at most schools, and users might make their objections very clearly known if the libraries were not open during such hours.

In many sci-tech libraries agreements have been made with departments of instruction to allow their faculty members and qualified graduate students to have keys to the library, or, alternatively, access to a key at a security station. In this way the departments may have after-hours access to the libraries involved. These users are reliable, they need to have access to the literature for longer hours than the library can economically stay open, and they are familiar enough with the collection to be able to function without staff assistance. Chemistry libraries are the most likely to have this arrangement, since chemists have such a need for the literature and since their experiments are often run on a round-the-clock basis. The disadvantage is that there are always a few individuals who will abuse such a privilege and take literature without charging it out properly. One has to weigh the desirability of such arrangements for the users against the possibilities of security problems.

Widely different practices are found in various universities. My survey found that at one university (Johns Hopkins), where there is only one library, it was open 365 days a year from 8:00 A.M. until midnight. There is also a nearby reading room open for five nights a week from 11:00 P.M. to 11:00 A.M., thus giving users twenty-four-hour use of facilities, with the library open sixteen of those hours.[4] The combined science library at the University of Georgia was found to be open until 2:00 A.M., as was the library at California Institute of Technology. In all these cases there was only one facility to staff, thereby reducing costs and enabling the merging of students from many backgrounds, versus the case of trying to keep many smaller libraries open for specific disciplines. It seemed that the universities with several sci-tech libraries had, on the average, hours from around 9:00 A.M. to 10:00 P.M. Monday through Thursday, usually closed Friday nights, and usually open on Saturday, but not often on Sunday.

A survey taken by a University of Maryland librarian of twenty-four university libraries devoted to physics, mathematics, engineering, or combinations of these subjects found the average library open 74 hours per week, with a range from 42 to 112 hours.[5] About two-thirds were open seven days a week, one-fourth were closed on Sunday but open on Saturdays, and one-eighth were closed both Saturday and Sunday. Over half the libraries issued keys, usually to faculty members and graduate students. The libraries which issued keys were all under fifty thousand volumes in size and only one was an engineering library, the rest being either physics libraries or mathematics libraries. The libraries which issued keys were open an average of sixty-nine hours per week versus eighty hours for those not issuing keys. So the pattern in the survey seems to be that the larger the library the less likely it would be to issue keys, but that the hours would be longer than in those issuing keys. A library not issuing keys typically was open weekdays until 11:00 P.M. while those issuing keys closed, on the average, at 9:00 P.M.

Each university must make its own decisions on these matters. If the use of the library seems low at any given hour or season, it is wise to have the desk attendant at each library in question take a head count of the patrons on hand, usually with hourly intervals frequent enough. Such a survey is often worth hours of speculation about how many users there are at a given time period; taking the survey is quick and direct evidence of conditions. It should be taken over long enough periods, however, to avoid nontypical conditions such as bad weather, vacations, and holidays. No publicity should be given the survey so as to avoid abnormal use patterns.

On the other hand, a study of the number and hourly habits of users can develop into a rather sizable survey. A report which is now mainly of interest because of the techniques used, rather than its findings, was based on a study of conditions at MIT by Nicholson and Bartlett.[6] Part of the findings included a study of use patterns for each hour the libraries were open, with over eight thousand users participating in the one-week survey.

Closely related to the topic of circulation services in general is that of the delivery of requested items to users, particularly faculty members. Those campuses where sci-tech libraries are consolidated into one unit are much more likely to offer this service than schools having several small libraries close to the departments primarily serviced. Service is usually restricted to faculty members to keep it within the bounds of the staff available. Some universities providing this service make one delivery per weekday, usually to a central point in the buildings served, such as a departmental office. Others give more personal service, going directly to a professor's office. Each campus is apt to present different reactions to this plan, with such variables as size of campus, number of library units, and faculty interest affecting the outcome. An account of how it is handled by science libraries at the University of Virginia is found in an article by Pancake.[7]

Reference Services

This section will discuss interlibrary loans, reader assistance in answering inquiries, preparation of bibliographies, use of computerized data bases, and instructional activities involving the library. In some circles these have been known as reader services; the name may vary but the activities are the same.

Interlibrary Loans—It is a long-standing custom to help inquirers obtain loans from other libraries, providing that a member of the library's group of users needs the material and providing that there is a likely source for the requested item. It is usually a waste of time to attempt to borrow certain materials, such as extremely rare items, reference books, or materials in delicate condition. Traditionally, the larger libraries lend many more items per year than they borrow, so it is a case of the larger libraries carrying the major burden of the expense of the system. A study made by Kaser showed that sixty libraries in the United States made around 70 percent of the interlibrary loans, with some large libraries spending as much as $100,000 per year handling outside requests.[8] Clearly this situation cannot go on forever. For some years the question of how to finance this process has been discussed, with charges for loans given serious consideration. New York State supports a system whereby its libraries can borrow from a network of libraries within the state, with the loaning library being given a payment for handling a request and a larger fee for making a loan. The NYSILL system, as it is known, is certainly a help but it only shows the need for a national system, as Kaser aptly points out.

Some universities restrict the obtaining of interlibrary loans to faculty members and graduate students; the reason is to hold the volume to a reasonable level.

It is standard practice to verify all requests with authoritative sources, to use ALA-approved forms in mailing ILL requests to another library, and to require the borrower to use the material in the borrowing library area, to insure its safety. Volumes should of course be returned promptly, with adequate insurance and proper wrapping. In the event of any damage which can be deemed the borrower's fault, settlement should take place quickly. Adherence to these simple rules is crucial to the smooth running of interlibrary loan programs.

Librarians in sci-tech libraries need to be adept at deciphering abbreviations of periodical titles in references sought by patrons, since so many ILLs in those libraries involve periodicals. In identifying titles of periodicals, if all-purpose union lists fail to help, it is often worthwhile to use the lists of periodicals indexed by major sci-tech indexing services, such as *Chemical Abstracts, Engineering Index,* or *Science Citation Index.* A variation on this procedure is to check author indexes for the appropriate years in pertinent indexing services in order to find the reference.

Many libraries prefer to send a few pages of photocopies rather than lend entire bound volumes, or, in the event the article desired is too long to copy gratis, to charge the would-be borrower for a photocopy. However, this should be done only if the borrower agrees, either in advance or upon notification. Once again the question of copyrights comes up when photocopies are mentioned, but at least university libraries are charging rates to cover expenses and not to make a profit.

Reference Questions—As any practicing librarian knows, reference questions can range from simple directional questions to complicated inquiries that might take days of searching to answer. In the case of faculty members, it is perfectly legitimate for the library staff to devote long hours of work if the overall staff schedule permits. Usually schedules do not allow for unlimited searching; when time is running out, some compromise or alternate means of helping a faculty member must be sought. As for students, the library staff should not get involved in doing the students' work for them. If the class assignment is to find a particular bit of information, the librarian should merely help the students learn how to search and should not find it for them. At the other end of the spectrum of student requests, it would be equally out of place for a library staff member to search for a suitable dissertation topic for a graduate student. This is a task the student must do.

One of the rules in doing reference work is to be sure the question is clearly and accurately stated before any time is spent on it. My article in *Special Libraries* on the patrons' difficulties in posing accurate questions lists nine reasons why the question as originally stated may be far from the one that should have been asked.[9] Reference librarians should be aware of this problem so as to take proper steps to remedy the situation.

In order to do reference work efficiently, the reference librarian must keep constantly aware of new tools or changes in old ones. This is difficult to do if one does not use familiar sources frequently. There is much to be said for making a periodic round of reference tools and glancing through the latest editions or issues in order to spot important changes.

Sometimes reference work will involve finding out one specific item of information, such as the melting point of a compound, the design of a particular electronic circuit, or a description of the geological features of a special region. On the other hand, some reference questions cannot be answered by a simple factual statement, particularly when the literature on the subject may be contradictory or unclear. In this case the librarian must make a judgment as to what is worth showing the patron and what is not. The degree of selectivity used in choosing items to show the requester depends on how much material is available on a topic. If searching turns up only a few borderline references, these are pointed out if there is nothing better. If there is much material available, however, selections can be made on the basis of such criteria as date of publication, status of the author or publisher of the data, and presence of annotated references in an article.

Another variable in the process of doing research is the type of service desired by the patron. Herner's well-known analysis of the ways in which scientists and engineers gather information states that those in the pure sciences are more apt to want to do their own bibliographic searches, whereas the applied scientist prefers to have his bibliographic searches done for him.[10] This study of over six hundred persons at Johns Hopkins University also showed that pure scientists relied on the libraries more and spent more time there than did the applied scientists. Much has been written on the habits of sci-tech personnel in regard to library services, and continued research on this important topic is needed. A more recent survey of the informational needs and library attitudes of five hundred physicists showed that they regard printed literature as their chief source.[11] It describes their journal preferences, their use patterns of libraries, and their degree of success in libraries.

Bibliographies—In preparing bibliographies, the reference librarian should ascertain how the patron wants the data arranged—whether alphabetically by author, chronologically by date of publication, by broad subjects, and so forth. If annotations or abstracts are desired, a decision must be made on how much thoroughness is required. Annotations can range from those which merely summarize the highlights of a piece of literature (an indicative abstract) to those which give very detailed information (an informative abstract). Naturally the informative type is more demanding and hence more time-consuming to prepare; it is quite likely that the requester does not need nor want such elaborate annotations.

In the rare case of a university librarian having enough time to prepare a very thorough investigation of all types of literature, including patents, obscure journals, pamphlets, or preprints, a literature search is called for. This procedure, the ultimate in reference work, is not done lightly for it requires a great amount of time. Generally, more than casual annotations are required, and the searcher must be able to distinguish the quality of the various items located. Facility with foreign languages is also a frequent requirement.

SDI and Computer Searches—Some libraries perform various types of current awareness services for researchers, known by the general term of selective dissemination of literature (SDI). If done manually, the time involved usually requires that only certain key journals or a very narrow subject be searched.

An alternative has become available in the past decade or so—namely, computerized searching of data bases to match detailed profiles of the requester's interests. There are many data bases in machine-readable form available now, usually on magnetic tape. They are produced by professional societies (such as the American Chemical Society, or the American Society for Metals), by commercial publishers (such as the Institute of Scientific Information), or by government agencies (such as the National Technical Information Service). One fairly detailed survey of the commercially available data bases of this type is that done by Schneider and others.[12] It presents the subject scope, type of data covered, tape specifications, and other features for eighty-one data bases. A directory of data bases centered on the physical sciences, as well as service bureaus, is available in a periodical article.[13]

Most universities do not have the funds to obtain tapes for all the subjects of interest to their scientists and engineers. Besides the costs of leasing tapes, the expenses of handling and searching them are considerable. On the other hand, making experimental studies of the best utilization of particular tape services, or finding out how university sci-tech researchers react to computerized SDI service or related studies, may very well be appropriate for a university sci-tech library. An example is the study made of SPIN (Searchable Physics Information Notices) tapes by New York University, as reported by Teitelbaum.[14] This study describes the problems of initiating the service, and covers cost figures and means of evaluation.

In recent years two new services have entered the picture, namely, for-profit and not-for-profit service bureaus which subscribe to many tape services and offer SDI and retrospective searching to interested users for a fee. The not-for-profit agencies are generally connected with a university, yet offer services on a national basis. Operational characteristics of such centers are discussed in the article by Park, based partly upon the features of the unit offering such services at the University of Georgia.[15] Number of data bases handled, cost factors, timeliness, and user profiles are some of the topics covered.

One of the outstanding features of certain for-profit service bureaus is the availability of on-line service. This means that all users may use their own terminals on which to request data and receive printed responses. Many modern terminals use cathode ray systems so that the printing is electronic and completely noiseless. For those who have their own terminals, the cost of a search can be in the neighborhood of $5 or so for ten minutes, but a lot of data can be retrieved in this short time. It is no longer necessary to have minimum length contracts with service bureaus now that charges can be made on a per-use basis.

Most experienced librarians recommend that a library staff member be the one to use the terminal on behalf of the requester, since doing searches at a terminal quickly and efficiently requires a considerable learning period. Requesters could get discouraged if their first attempt at using a terminal was not satisfactory due to their own inexperience. Maier's article stresses the librarian's role in familiarizing scientists with computerized services.[16]

It is common practice for service bureaus to airmail complete references and abstracts to requesters, once desired partial references have been selected on-line at the terminal. This reduces the overall cost of a search since it frees the terminal from being used merely as a printing device, which is a rather inefficient use of it.

Experience has also shown that many engineers and scientists are wary of the value of computer searching of data bases. They may feel that they are already covering the literature well in their own manual searching routines, or they have little confidence in the ability of the computer to locate pertinent items for them, or they cannot afford computer searching. Each case is a separate one, and often word-of-mouth reports of success by one user is the best way to get others interested.

One factor which affects the success of SDI systems (in which a requester signs up for searching on the topics of interest to him over a fixed period of time), is the care with which the requester's interests have been analyzed and coded for the computer to search. This codification is called the profile of the patron's interests. The profile often needs adjustment after the first few searches have been made and it then becomes apparent whether the profile was too broad, too narrow, or used the wrong terms. Preparing a good profile requires knowledge of the subject and of general search techniques.

The librarian, as well as the research worker or faculty member who has never used a computerized search, may well ask what advantages such a system has over manual searching. A complete answer is rather lengthy, but the general reasons can be given here.

One point that many computer centers may or may not make is that sometimes it is better to use a printed index rather than a computer. This is especially true when all that is needed is to check an author's name or one simple subject, without complicating side issues. On the other hand, computers can search more quickly than humans when there are several subjects to correlate. For example, searches which involve three subjects (e.g., the welding of underwater steel plates, or alcoholism of female rats) can be done much more quickly by computer than manually. This assumes that the indexing done for the data base has been done in enough detail to allow the retrieval of important points.

Another advantage of computer-based SDI services is that the number of periodicals covered can be much larger than that covered by a librarian and can be searched with no problems of fatigue or lessened interest. Of course, subtle points that a computer would not notice would be apparent to a skilled researcher. Yet the advantages of computer searching over manual are many.

Those desiring information on the programs for computer-based information systems at six universities are referred to a study made by the National Bureau of Standards.[17] Design considerations, operational characteristics, and other factors are discussed.

No doubt in the years ahead computers will play an ever-increasing role in the reference services offered at universities. To date much more is available in machine-readable data bases for the sciences than for the social sciences or humanities. For that reason alone, then, it is important for sci-tech librarians to keep abreast of this important field.

There is not a great amount of information on the relative costs of manual versus on-line computerized searches, but an article by Elman offers data on using one of the commercial data bases offering on-line service.[18] Actual dollar amounts are given, with computerized searching claimed to be much cheaper than the manual method.

Instructional Programs—One area of service being given increased attention by college and university libraries is that of instructional services. This refers to activities designed to widen students', faculty members', and research staff members' knowledge of the use of libraries. The service may range from a simple tour of the facilities to a course given for credit in the use of science or engineering literature. The ultimate goal is to make the library patrons more skilled and efficient in their use of information sources. Quite often even faculty members are woefully ignorant as to the reference tools, abstracting services, and other valuable sources of data available in their library. Students are usually ignorant of all but the most common tools.

The topic, instructional programs, is not new to collegiate library circles, but it is gaining recognition as an area deserving of more attention than it has received in the past. A survey by Griffin and Clarke of twenty large university libraries, in regard to their orientation and instructional programs for users, discusses the various activities and evaluates their success.[19]

Several universities in recent years have appointed staff members whose primary responsibility is to coordinate the activity of the library staff in its instructional programs. Such steps will help insure that more attention and creative effort are given to these projects.

One of the simplest projects is to prepare printed guides describing library collections, services, and hours. These guides should not be too comprehensive; the use of colorful, attractive paper and layouts is recommended to increase their appeal to readers. If the library is at all complicated, a map might well be included, showing where blocks of materials are kept, such as reference books, reserve items, and journals, as well as the location of photocopying equipment, microform readers, and other special tools.

Another relatively uncomplicated service is to offer tours of the library to users, as staff time permits. Although the beginning of a semester or term, particularly in the fall, is the most popular time for tours, they should be offered periodically throughout the year if possible. They can be advertised through posters, bulletin board announcements, and notices in campus newspapers. In addition free bookmarks inexpensively printed can be distributed to advertise the tours, or letters may be sent to new graduate students and new faculty members.

Tours are easier to offer if the group is homogeneous in background, so that the comments can be readily geared to their needs. The more diverse the backgrounds of those on hand for the tour, the more general the information will have to be. However, certain highlights must be brought out, such as basic facts on the type and size of the collection, the general circulation policies, types of reference books (especially the names of the major periodical indexes and other items of particular importance in the library), and special services offered. In a chemistry library, for example, a tour should point out the location of works such as Beilstein, and in a library containing technical reports, the location of the report indexes and the microform readers, if any.

Through lectures to classes, to groups of new graduate students, or to other groups librarians can give more detailed instruction in the use of the library. Good relations with faculty members will help increase the opportunity to present such lectures, and in time they may become a regular part of the routine of the professors involved or of the school orientation program. The talks should be carefully prepared, with the needs of the students clearly in mind.

At some universities sci-tech librarians teach courses, given for credit, that deal with the nature and use of science or engineering literature. Such a course at Columbia University is required for certain types of engineers, and is optional for all others; an average of twenty students take it each semester. The course covers the characteristics of different types of literature, such as patents, handbooks, technical reports, and how the types are best used, as well as common library tools, including the card catalog and microform readers. Assignments are based on a technical topic selected by each student.

Graduate students often need such courses more than undergraduates, in view of the research required in most advanced programs. Yet it is harder to make library instruction a regular part of their programs. Perhaps an introductory lecture at the start of the year is the best one can hope for until faculty support is built up to make a full-fledged credit-granting course a possibility.

Those desiring a comparison of different types of library instruction (live versus tape, for example) are referred to the article by Kuo.[20] Instruction for students in introductory biology is described in Kirk's article.[21] Two types of instruction are compared.

Access and Security—These topics have some points in common since the losses of library collections are related to having users present, particularly at times when staffing is light and security precautions may be at a minimum.

Almost every type of library is having problems with users taking books, mutilating them, or otherwise disregarding library rules. Some libraries have been driven to using electronic detection systems, which unfortunately are not always effective. One brand, for example, cannot distinguish between a book and a briefcase, thus causing many false alarms.

Another system requires that all books be sensitized at least once during a charge-out or a return to the library cycle; this system is cumbersome. A new type of detection system, which is said to involve the use of tiny printed circuits, supposedly has none of the disadvantages of either system.

Many sci-tech librarians have found that their students have the technical know-how to outwit many security systems; one should therefore not expect any system to be permanently fool-proof.

Other librarians contend that the way to bring about improvements in security is to stress to students that they are only harming themselves when volumes are not properly charged out and returned, since money for replacing missing volumes invariably comes from the funds for purchasing new works. Unfortunately, this does not have much significance to some students.

One inexpensive plan to reduce losses is to have briefcases checked at the door, whether in coin-return lockers which cost the students nothing or at the circulation desk where desk attendants handle them. It is more difficult to conceal books in clothing, for example, than in a bag or briefcase, so libraries with unacceptable losses are urged to try checking bags at the door.

Some libraries which allow faculty members and graduate students to have keys for access to the library after it is closed have not experienced losses as severe as units which do not issue keys. It is primarily a matter of local pride or respect for the collection which seems to control the situation. The smaller the library and the smaller the group it serves, the more successful the use of keys as far as security is concerned. Chemistry libraries often seem to fare better than those in other disciplines. Such libraries usually serve discrete, specialized groups, linked by a common respect for the value of the literature.

Librarians still have much to learn about user attitudes and habits if they are to improve security conditions in their libraries.

Notes

[1]Jerold Nelson, "Faculty Awareness and Attitudes toward Academic Library Reference Services: A Measure of Communication." *College & Research Libraries* 34, no. 5 (September 1973): 268-275.

[2]Ellis Mount, *University Science and Engineering Libraries—A Survey*, September 1972, 26 p. (Available from ERIC Document Reproduction Service, Bethesda, Maryland, 20014, as ED 068 108.)

[3]Morrison C. Haviland, "Loans to Faculty Members in University Libraries," *College & Research Libraries* 28, no. 3 (May 1967): 171-174.

[4]Mount, *University Science.*

[5]University of Maryland, Engineering and Physical Sciences Library, *Report of Survey*, Compiled by Richard W. Frenier (College Park, Md., 1974), 4 p.

[6]Natalie N. Nicholson, and Eleanor Bartlett. "Who Uses University Libraries?" *College & Research Libraries* 23, no. 3 (May 1962): 217-222, 257-259.

[7]Edwina H. Pancake, "Intra-library Science Information Service," *Special Libraries* 64, nos. 5/6 (May/June 1973): 228-234.

[8]David Kaser, "Whither Interlibrary Loan?," *College & Research Libraries* 33, no. 5 (September 1972): 398-402.

[9]Ellis Mount, "Communication Barriers and the Reference Question," *Special Libraries* 57, no. 8 (October 1966): 575-578.

[10]Saul Herner, "Information Gathering Habits of Workers in Pure and Applied Science," *Industrial and Engineering Chemistry* 46, no. 1 (January 1954): 228-236.

[11]Ching-chih Chen, "How Do Scientists Meet Their Information Needs?" *Special Libraries* 65, no. 7 (July 1974): 272-280.

[12]John H. Schneider and others, *Survey of Commercially Available Computer-readable Bibliographic Data Bases* (Washington, D.C.: American Society for Information Science, 1973), 181 p.

[13]Lindsay Murdock and Olivia Opello. "Computer Literature Searches in the Physical Sciences," *Special Libraries* 64, no. 10 (October 1973): 442-445.

[14]Priscilla Teitelbaum, "Case History on Use of SPIN (Searchable Physics Information Notices) Tapes for Current Awareness Service," *ASIS Proceedings* 10 (1973): 227-228.

[15]Margaret K. Park, "Computer-based Bibliographic Retrieval Services: The View from the Center," *Special Libraries* 64, no. 4 (April 1973): 187-192.

[16]Joan M. Maier, "The Scientist versus Machine Search Services: We Are the Missing Link," *Special Libraries* 65, no. 4 (April 1974): 180-188.

[17]Beatrice Marron and others. *A Study of Six University-based Information Systems* (Washington, D.C.: U.S. National Bureau of Standards, 1973). 1 vol. (NBS Technical Note 781.)

[18]Stanley A. Elman. "Cost Comparison of Manual and On-Line Computerized Literature Searching." *Special Libraries* 66, no. 1 (January 1975): 12-18.

[19]Lloyd Griffin and Jack A. Clarke, "Orientation and Instruction of Graduate Students in the Use of the University Library: A Survey," *College & Research Libraries* 33, no. 6 (November 1972): 467-472.

[20]Frank F. Kuo, "A Comparison of Six Versions of Science LibraryiInstruction," *College & Research Libraries* 34, no. 4 (July 1973): 287-290.

[21]Thomas Kirk, "A Comparison of Two Methods of Library Instruction for Students in Introductory Biology." *College & Research Libraries* 32, no. 6 (November 1971): 465-474.

8

Relationships with Other Groups

Like most organizations in our society, an individual sci-tech library at a university has relationships with a complicated array of other groups, some of which are more important to its operation than others. In order to understand such libraries well, it is useful to describe their position in regard to other organizations and groups.

Some of the groups are not formally organized, with group members having perhaps nothing more in common than being undergraduate students in the subject(s) served by the library. Some are closely related to the library, such as other libraries in the same university system. Others are very remotely connected with the library in terms of distance, yet may influence its operations to a large extent, as exemplified by the Library of Congress.

In this chapter a brief summary will be given of the significance of these various groups to the operation and characteristics of sci-tech libraries.

Library Users

There are three main groups of sci-tech library users, namely, the faculty, students (undergraduate and graduate), and members of the research staff.

Faculty Members—Of all the user groups at a university, faculty members are the most cohesive, and are capable of making a major impression on a library's style of operation. If faculty members are pleased with the library, they may not be heard from. If they are not pleased, their influence is often such that they can remedy situations to their liking.

This is not to say that faculty influence is unlimited. If the library budget for the university is half what it should be, all that faculty members may be able to do is to inform the administration of their displeasure and thereby cause some modest increases. But if hours, circulation rules, and the like do not measure up to their expectations, it is not uncommon for them to have serious discussions with the library administrators. Just solutions require tact and skill on the part of administrators. The librarians and faculty members can feel equally insistent that their views are right. Many times a compromise is best, unless a major point of basic policy is at stake. For less important points, a spirit of give and take is recommended.

Faculty members can often serve as allies to the library staff if the university administration does not cooperate well with the library system—for example, if the administration does not grant reasonable funds and facilities for the system. It requires discretion in such matters to avoid a confrontation between conflicting views, but strong faculty support is always helpful to a cause.

Many faculty members are avid users of the library, and some rarely use it. Some regularly suggest new literature for the library, and others give it no attention. Like any other group, they are individuals with distinct differences of habits. One of the tasks of a librarian is to try to make them all regular library users.

Students—Students, particularly undergraduates, are a far less cohesive group than faculty members. They are not as involved with the library, they are usually around for just a few years, and they are so large a group as to be very divergent in their views and needs. The exceptions are graduate students, particularly those within a given department, who, with their common interests, are bound close together; sometimes they can speak with as much solidarity of interest as faculty members.

It should not be surprising to learn that graduate students are probably the heaviest group of users at a university library, even outdistancing the faculty. A survey of a large university library system showed that 49 percent of the items checked out of the system were borrowed by graduate students, while 59 percent of those items used in the library were for this group.[1] Fifty percent of those receiving reference service were graduates. So the needs of graduate students must be kept in mind in planning library operations. For example, many of them stay at a university year round, with intersession periods having little meaning to their life-style. Therefore, a library system which, for example, makes libraries unavailable for long periods of time, for whatever reason, is not considering the needs of graduate students.

Undergraduates generally use the less complex materials in a research library, although there are, of course, many exceptional students at this level who avidly seek advanced materials. On the average, however, their needs are generally met by reserve materials and similar instructional items. But the literary taste of the graduate student may be almost identical to that of some faculty members. So while there are levels of sophistication among users, graduate students, particularly those at the doctoral and postdoctoral level, are frequently on a par with faculty members in terms of advanced materials.

Research Staff—These people are the least known of the three groups, but are closest to faculty members in their literary needs. They, too, are most interested in research materials. They are often employed on a year-round basis, thus giving them an interest in library schedules similar to those of graduate students. Most of them have graduate degrees and excellent skills in their disciplines, but politically their influence on a campus is not nearly as great as that of the instructional staff. While no librarian should make policies and plans on the basis of popularity polls or on an estimate of what can be accepted by any group without grumbling, it is well to know which groups can exert the most political pressures. In this way should differences of opinion arise over library policies and procedures, the librarian will be prepared.

Library Committees—A library needs a library committee for several reasons, the most important of which is to provide a means of communication with users so that the library administration can learn their attitudes on important matters. In a sense the committee can serve as a safety valve, so that differences between users and the libraries can be resolved before conditions get too serious. A secondary purpose is to try out ideas on them as a sounding board, since most librarians prefer to have some idea of user reaction before making significant changes.

Both faculty members and students should be on the committee if possible, so that the viewpoints of both groups are heard. Since department heads or deans traditionally appoint faculty members to committees, the inclusion of students is a matter to be taken up with the committees. If the committee agrees to student members—and that is now not an unusual situation—then the department head or dean can find the means to name student members. Student councils are often good sources of names of likely members.

The larger the committee, the more important it is to have a regular order for meetings, with minutes, agendas, and the like, whereas small two- or three-member committees can afford to be more casual in their meetings. There are differences of opinion about whether the librarian should serve as chairman or whether a chairman should be elected.

Other University Library Units

It is obvious that some units within a university library system will have much closer ties to sci-tech units than others, and further, that patterns of close relationships vary from one sci-tech unit to another. Perhaps of all those in the sci-tech group only an engineering library would have close relationships with an architecture library, whereas only the geology library might be closely tied to the geography department. Mutual interests in acoustics could be one tie between a physics library and a music library, and a joint concern about applied electronics might link a music library with an engineering library. The role of science in society might be a matter of common interest for both a general science library and one devoted to social sciences.

The point is that there are no hard, distinct boundary lines separating the sci-tech libraries from their nontechnical fellow library units at a university, just as the sci-tech libraries themselves have many overlapping fields of interest. For many reasons the librarians in all units should be cognizant of the activities of other units, even those which are normally of little mutual interest. One way of accomplishing this is by meetings of professional staff members of all units, at which topics of general interest are discussed. Another is by the formation of task forces or committees to study topics or activities that affect all libraries, such as improved reference work, with membership cutting across all subject areas. By working closely with other librarians, one learns to understand their problems and viewpoints, which tends to unify a library system, even one with a far-flung group of specialized units.

This is not to say that different disciplines do not need different services or different types of collections. The sci-tech units, for example, would require large collections of periodicals as compared to, say, a philosophy library, where old monographs might be the most important part of its collection. A chemistry library might be prudent to allow faculty members and graduate students to have after-hours access to the library because of on-going experiments, whereas a journalism library, for example, would have no need for such access.

Another means of cooperation between libraries is a union list of serials for related libraries. It might mean that a given library's titles would be listed in more than one subject grouping. Serials in a psychology library, for example, might well be listed in a sci-tech union list as well as in one for the social sciences. Seminars on uses of computerized data bases are now of interest to many disciplines, with the growing number of data bases outside the sci-tech area. Personnel management is another topic without meaningful boundaries, since the problems of orientation, training, and work standards are very similar in all libraries.

Other Library Systems

No library system can exist completely independent of all other libraries. There are many reasons for this interdependence, one being that no one system has all the material its users will need. This is becoming more and more a reason for library cooperation, especially as costs of literature continue to rise and library budgets continue to constrict. Libraries are seeking different ways to solve their problems through cooperation, such as cooperative cataloging, agreements on collection policies, or enhanced means of accommodating loan requests and/or borrowers from each other's campuses.

Just in collections alone, libraries can do much to minimize costs of storing literature or to reduce costs of acquisitions. The practice of two universities in the same geographical area keeping the same rarely used periodicals or monographs constitutes a waste of valuable space that can no longer be tolerated. But until economic pressures compel them to enter cooperative agreements, little is likely to happen. Hopefully, they would enter into agreements, study their mutual collections, arrive at sensible patterns of discard, and establish practical means for sharing little-used materials. The same mutuality of interest should govern their acquisition of expensive, little-used new materials. This would not mean that they would discontinue purchasing items needed regularly for instruction, for example, or heavily used research items. Instead it would enable them to diversify their purchase of special research items rather than having both buy the same unusual new item when one would suffice. The money saved by relying on the other library could thus be used to purchase items that previously were financially impossible.

There are good indications that many people in the publishing world do not understand how this kind of cooperation operates. Many publishers are fearful that basic materials will no longer be duplicated on each campus or that the market for major research items will shrink. However, they might well consider the realities of the situation, as described above, to see that the net effect could well be beneficial for the publishing world. No library is going to give up materials it needs constantly, no matter how many libraries it is cooperating with. But its reliance on other libraries could well give it the funds to purchase special items it might not otherwise be able to afford.

There have been several projects to set up nationwide repositories of various types, such as the translation pool maintained by the John Crerar Library in Chicago. It has its own monthly index, and will accept donations of translations from all sources to supplement its regular acquisitions of established translation series. Sometimes the effort is on a regional level, such as regional collections of technical reports. One set for a multistate region, with fast means of copying or prompt mail service to reach requesters quickly, is probably sufficient. For example, the collection of around two-thirds of a million technical reports at Columbia University not only serves the metropolitan New York area but also reaches users in at least three other states.

The Center for Research Libraries is currently operating a federally funded experiment to determine if it could subscribe to certain very rare titles and thus relieve member libraries of the costs of subscribing, cataloging, and handling these periodicals.

Other examples of library cooperation include the consortium recently formed (consisting of the New York Public Library and the libraries at Harvard, Yale, and Columbia) known as the Research Libraries Group. Goals of this group are to coordinate collection development policies of the four libraries and to share resources in practical ways. Library networks, including the well-known OCLC shared cataloging operation, are gaining in popularity.

Another common method of cooperation is between a university and a local scientific or technical organization, such as a science museum with a strong library in certain disciplines. The university might well eliminate much of its purchase of little-used materials in those fields and rely on the museum, through the means of speedy interlibrary loan service or other procedures. In some cases the universities have even paid for subscriptions for materials to be processed and housed at a nearby cooperating institution.

Industrial, Commercial, and Governmental Organizations

For many years industries and business organizations have relied on university libraries for materials not in their own special libraries, most of which are relatively small compared to university collections. The interlibrary loan service or the purchase of single photocopies has been the normal way to satisfy their needs. While universities have sometimes benefited from this in the form of developing good public relations or receiving an occasional gift of funds, in general they probably spend money they can ill afford to provide such service. Only rarely do these small libraries have materials needed by the universities, so it is mostly a one-way street as far as the direction in which materials are loaned.

Some universities, such as Stanford and Georgia Tech, have adopted the plan of establishing separate units within the library organization to deal specifically with such users. They also have a fee plan to reimburse themselves for the services rendered. A detailed description of the operation of the system at Georgia Tech may be found in the article by Dodd, which describes the handling of interlibrary loans, photocopying, and computer-based searches.[2] University libraries that receive heavy requests for their materials from business and industry might well consider the solution Dodd proposes. These special libraries seem particularly interested in sci-tech materials rather than in those from the humanities or social sciences. (The exceptions are business and legal items, which also receive a lot of interest from outside groups.)

Most universities have contracts and grants from governmental agencies. Generally, the libraries of the university are to serve those working on the grants as well as those working on strictly instructional or unsponsored research. The libraries do figure in the computation of the overhead rate charged outside agencies by the university, since portions of the cost of maintaining a research library system are properly recognized as one of the legitimate charges for sponsored research. It was partially for the purpose of trying to determine which portion of library costs could be charged to research and which to instructional purposes that the previously cited study of research costs at Columbia University Libraries was conducted.[3] At that time the research uses were found to require around 64 percent of the library budget and 63 percent of the space the libraries occupied, with the remainder in each case related to instructional activities.

Some universities have operated libraries for governmental agencies in cases where the agencies are on or near the campus, with all costs reimbursed. As long as the goals of the agencies and the university coincide, there is apt to be little cause for friction. However, in recent years campus unrest and other causes have led to a reevaluation of the prudence of such relationships and, in some cases, to cancellation of contracts with the agency. In other cases no problem arose because of the nature of the agencies involved.

Library and Other Professional Organizations

The relationship of libraries to library organizations depends in large part upon their individual professional staff members whose efforts on behalf of the organizations serve to tie them to the universities. This situation is very changeable since the interests of other librarians succeeding previously heavily involved staff members may be very different. Some librarians feel it is their responsibility to further the work of professional library groups, while others take little or no part in such groups. Personal reasons are often so compelling that participation in professional groups may be impossible. Others may feel shy, or lazy, or too busy to get involved. While staff members may go overboard and devote too much time to library groups, administrators generally favor a reasonable amount of professional activity. The updating of knowledge, the development of leadership qualities, and the friendships developed all help the individual perform his duties. For example, reference questions can be answered more quickly by knowing whom to call in neighboring libraries; such knowledge if frequently gained by attending library society meetings.

To a lesser extent membership in technical or scientific societies benefits sci-tech librarians, particularly those closely related to the goals or subject areas of the libraries involved. Another reason for librarians to have personal memberships in such societies is that they might thereby save sizable publication costs. In many cases only individuals (normally the librarian) and not the institutions, can be accepted for membership.

Notes

[1]Ellis Mount and Paul Fasana, "An Approach to the Measurement of Use and Cost of a Large Academic Research Library System: A Report of a Study Done at Columbia University Libraries," *College & Research Libraries* 33, no. 3 (May 1972): 199-211.

[2]James B. Dodd, "Pay-As-You-Go Plan for Satellite Industrial Libraries Using Academic Facilities," *Special Libraries* 65, no. 2 (February 1974): 66-72.

[3]Mount and Fasana, "An Approach."

9

Library Facilities and Equipment

Much of the effectiveness of a library depends upon its physical facilities and equipment. Users tend to be very much aware of the comfort and attractiveness of the libraries they use. A fine collection and an excellent staff are both partially negated if the user is confronted with a dingy, poorly lighted reading area, with old, uncomfortable tables and chairs. A certain minimum quality of facilities is to be expected in a well-run library system. Opulence and splendor are neither required nor expected, but the layout, amount of space, equipment, and environmental aspects must be of a high enough quality to make the users and staff feel comfortable working there. This is merely part of the cost of running a university library system, and does not represent an unreasonable desire on the part of librarians for plush, expensive quarters.

It is a rare university librarian whose career will not include at least one exposure to the process of modernizing or upgrading library facilities and equipment. (The term equipment as used here includes furniture, stacks, floor coverings, and mechanical and electrical devices.) Perhaps less common is the experience of designing an entirely new facility. Nevertheless, many sci-tech librarians will have this assignment. This chapter will point out many of the pitfalls to avoid in the planning process as well as some important points to keep in mind during the process.

While no two libraries present quite the same problems, certain basic guidelines do have wide applicability to planning university libraries.

Basic Aspects of Planning

Whether a sci-tech librarian is involved in modernizing an existing library or designing a new one, certain basic considerations can help insure the success of the project. No list could possibly be inclusive enough to guarantee that all pitfalls had been highlighted and all major topics included, but the following discussion at least covers many of the most common problems in planning.

Preplanning—The prudent librarian is constantly thinking of ways to improve the library he or she is responsible for, or what would be desirable in a new one. Librarians should keep up to date with the literature and with manufacturers' wares, such as are shown at library conferences. Then, when a modernization plan or a new library is announced, the librarian doesn't have to start from scratch, mentally.

The Planning Team—A suitable team should be chosen, including the librarian(s) involved, a representative of the university space committee, an architect, and, if conditions warrant, a special consultant. If the project is more modest, such as a modernization of existing space, it is possible that librarians, working with knowledgeable university staff members, can handle the project alone. The team must work together with complete candor and consideration of the other person's point of view. There is no place on this team for a prima donna.

The Program—A carefully written plan of what is to be done must be prepared. It will discuss the purpose of the library, its relation to other library units, its expected rate of growth, the type and size of staff it will require, the type of users and their needs, the outlook for future expansion, and similar major points that have a drastic effect on what sort of library should be developed. Preparing a detailed program is not a quick task, as it requires lengthy discussions of many points. Staff members, library users, and anyone else who would be affected by the resulting library should be involved. In this connection, a reasonably wide group of knowledgeable people should be sought *before* a plan is adopted, for to have to do so later and then make necessary changes would be at a greater cost of time and money. This does not mean holding an open house on the subject, but does include making sure that all viewpoints of affected people are heard. Another major aid in creating a good program is to visit other new libraries and to learn from their experiences. In this way planning will be done from a broad background of awareness of other libraries.

Seeing other libraries makes much more of an impression than merely reading about them. I once visited a new industrial library which had part of its stacks on a mezzanine floor. However, no one involved in the planning of that library had remembered to make any provision for getting book trucks up to the mezzanine level, not even a dumbwaiter. This makes a vivid impression—to see a handsome library with this defect—so that repetition of that mistake would be impossible once one has seen it.

Space Requirements—So many variables affect space estimates that it is one of the most difficult planning problems to handle. Generally, some limitations are imposed upon the project; for example, there are rules as to the overall size of a new building, the size of a floor allotted to the library, or the size of a room granted a smaller library. Even with these dimensions known, however, important questions remain, e.g., what portion of space is for the collection, what amount is for the staff, how much is for hallways.

One of the basic questions is how much is to be allowed for growth of collections. For example, if finances require such strict limitations on the project that only five to ten years of growth are possible, the librarian at least knows what must be planned. If there is no limitation at the outset, discussions within the library administration should lead to some figure to use for preliminary planning purposes, such as to see what would be required to plan for twenty years of growth. In modernization projects, there are usually very obvious limitations in the form of the size of the existing room(s) available. It is more of an open question in planning a new library. Even then, an entire new building is seldom given over to a science-engineering library. Most of the time the library shares the building with departments of instruction, and occupies one or two floors or a portion of a floor.

Collection space depends a great deal on whether there can be storage areas for little-used materials nearby, or on the outlook for cooperative collection programs with other libraries in a consortium, or on the possibilities for storing much of the older materials on microforms. All of these factors must be considered in estimating the space requirements for a given number of years, going beyond the simple extrapolation of current collection growth rates for the required number of years. No one can predict the future infallibly, but the more one considers such factors the better the estimate will be. (If books are sent to storage, the methods discussed in Chapter 5 should prove useful.)

Likewise, space for users depends upon some idea of the trends of the growth of the department(s) served. This, too, is a difficult area insofar as it involves the future. Another variable is the percentage of seats required for a given subject discipline. The number required for a law school library might be much higher than for an engineering library, for example. So it is not wise merely to copy what some other library on the campus has done.

Staff space is probably the simplest of the three to estimate since very large staff increases, enough to offset prudent allowances for reasonable growth, rarely occur. Probably only a dramatic change in the services and duties expected of the staff would cause such an occurrence. Staff areas should be planned with a fairly generous space allotment per person, partly to allow them plenty of work space and partly to allow for future growth. The percentages of the staff space versus the total space for the library is not high, so large portions of the total space are not involved.

Layout—Choosing the best location for different elements of the library is a very important step towards creating a desirable place in which to work. For example, putting a noisy staff telephone or typewriter next to a table where users will be examining reference works or using indexes would be a poor arrangement. I have seen plans for new libraries that have more than four exits, thus creating permanent security problems and requiring the manning of unnecessary positions.

Planners usually call this the traffic problem. Librarians are urged to consider the effect of the placement of elements, such as catalogs, staff areas, restrooms, elevators, telephones, reference areas, mail delivery stations, and a host of other parts of the library, very carefully before the final layout is accepted. Trying to visualize oneself as a user and mentally "using" each portion of a library from a preliminary plan will often uncover errors before it is too late to change them. Likewise, imagining oneself as a staff member shelving books, helping patrons, or otherwise using the facilities will uncover problems.

One obvious principle to remember is to allow enough uncrowded space for the element being placed. For example, putting a card catalog so close to an aisle that users would block the aisle, particularly near a main entrance, would cause endless trouble. Space between tables must allow for chairs to be pulled out without hitting other chairs. Space for filing cabinets must allow for pulling out the drawers, and files must not block aisles or create a safety hazard when drawers are out.

Fortunately, there are checklists, with recommendations for space requirements, available in the literature. The monumental work by Metcalf includes an appendix with many formulas and tables useful for this purpose.[1] The Special Libraries Association publication on planning special libraries includes a detailed check list of this sort, prepared by Jeanette Rockwell and Jean Flegal.[2]

Stack Areas—In many cases stacks can also serve as space dividers; for example, the stacks can break up a large study area (which tends to become noisy) into smaller areas, thus creating more privacy and less noise in the smaller areas. Conversely, seating areas can be used to break up large banks of stacks, so as to give the reader a convenient place to examine materials without having to walk long distances to the regular seating area. Some authorities recommend that no single range of shelving be longer than eighteen feet (six sections) without an aisle. This eliminates much wasted effort in getting to the exact section desired.

Shelving journals separately from monographs is a question to be considered early in the planning stages, which means that rates of growth of each type of literature must be estimated if they will not be interfiled. It is generally a good idea to separate them. Likewise, shelving reference and reserve materials separately, the normal practice, calls for growth figures for both such materials.

Seating Areas—The types of seating must be given careful consideration. A prime consideration is to keep seating in small clusters in order to reduce noise from conversation and traffic. In addition, the traditional long tables familiar in older libraries are largely being replaced by individual study tables and carrels, although a few large tables with several chairs should be available both for handling wide materials (such as maps and oversize books) and for accommodating those who must confer at the table. The conference purpose, however, is best served by having two or three closed study rooms (with a glass window facing the entrance, for security's sake) for group studying as well as for typing. As previously mentioned, the amount of space for total seating purposes depends upon enrollment figures (past and future), proximity of study halls or other areas for students to use, number of faculty members, use habits of the discipline involved, and so forth. It is, of course, desirable to be able to plan to accommodate, as a minimum, the number of users on hand during a peak period, such as exam time, unless funds are not ample enough. Otherwise, when seating becomes tight a few times a year, libraries have ways of compensating, such as allowing reserve books to be checked out for a few hours rather than requiring them to be read in the library. Hopefully, such restricted conditions should not occur regularly; if they do, then the library space has obviously been planned on too skimpy a scale.

Staff Areas—The circulation desk must be adjacent to the exit, with only one exit for users aside from required emergency exists (which should be equipped with crash bars and alarm bells). By proper planning, in smaller libraries and even moderately sized ones it is possible to man the library at slow periods with one desk attendant. This requires that the card catalog, telephones, serial records, and other elements be close enough to allow easy access without losing sight of the desk. It means the attendant cannot leave the area to help patrons, but at least reasonable assistance can be given as long as the basic records are all within easy reach. The larger the number of sci-tech units on a campus, the more important it is to have this arrangement. In consolidated science libraries one person would probably not be enough anyhow, so it becomes of little importance. However, the convenient access of the staff to the basic records must not be overlooked.

With the growing number of electrical devices for staff areas, including those at the circulation counter, the planner must be sure an abundance of electrical outlets is well distributed in the area. If an electronic book detection system is being considered, it is more satisfactory to design the circulation desk with that in mind. It becomes much more costly to have to do it as an afterthought.

Space for Audiovisual Aids; Computer Equipment; Copiers—Careful thought must be given to the needs of the library for areas where projectors, phonographs, video units, and the like can be used. Some disciplines, such as medicine, are currently much further along in the use of audiovisual aids as instructional materials, but hopefully this will not always be the case, with other disciplines catching up in time. There are many special considerations for housing materials of this sort, including power outlets, type of lighting, and control of outside distractions. Microform readers, now much more popular and more likely to be required for certain materials than ever before, also need care in planning. Unlike earlier units, newer models can operate in fairly bright light.

In the last few years the growth of on-line computerized data bases, both on-campus and off-campus, has made provision for a computer terminal a prudent part of planning. Neither the amount of space nor the electrical requirement is a difficult problem. However, it is not always easy to find a location that will allow good staff control of the terminal without putting it right in the midst of a noisy clerical operation. Users must be able to work alongside the staff member in charge of it, and some isolation from the rest of the staff is desirable. Yet it should not be so far away from the central staff area that control over the terminal becomes a problem.

A related problem is the location of photocopy units—some are rather noisy and many require special wiring. Depending upon the outcome of the copyright situation, visual control over what is copied may become more crucial; otherwise, with coin-operated units, the copiers can well be in isolated locations.

Miscellaneous Space Requirements—Except possibly in the warmest climates, provision for users' coats and rainwear is a very desirable asset. A practical reason for including lockers is to make it simpler for users to leave briefcases there. This increases the security of the library, since removing books illegally is simpler using briefcases, even when electronic security devices are used. The staff's storage area must be large enough for their coats and rainwear, as well as supplies of clerical materials and the like.

In libraries that have more than one floor, the elevators must be large enough to accommodate book trucks. Doors, which are normally equipped with alarm bells, must have cutoff switches to eliminate false alarms when book trucks are brought in through them. Mail and supplies should be brought into the library through a service entrance rather than the main door.

The head of the library, if he or she supervises a number of librarians, should have an office large enough to include a conference table, a blackboard, and enough wall outlets for use of audiovisual aids at the table.

Selection of Equipment and Furnishings

Even a mediocre plan for a library can seem less bothersome to users if the furnishings are attractive and well-designed. Poorly chosen equipment and furnishings, however, can spoil the effect of a well-designed library. The ideal, of course, is to have excellence in both facilities and equipment.

Environmental Features—These pertain to heating and ventilating as well as lighting. Since they are all highly specialized subjects, the librarian may not feel competent enough to specify what is needed along these lines. Yet, there are certain basic principles involved which, when understood, would enable the librarian to spot obvious problems and to ask intelligent questions of the planning team. The librarian should specify what is needed, and then let the specialists choose the best method of reaching the goals set.

In spite of the greater reliability of modern air conditioning equipment, it does break down occasionally. People who have had to work in buildings with windows that cannot be opened when air conditioning units are being repaired can vouch for the need for some way to ventilate space in an emergency.

Readers desiring more information on this subject are referred to a chapter in Metcalf's book and to a chapter by Ellsworth Mason in the collection edited by Weber.[3]

Fire Protection—Most writers on the subject recommend smoke detectors, not sprinklers, since water damage can ruin a library collection. Local ordinances vary as to the possibility of eliminating sprinklers. Metcalf devotes several pages to a discussion of both fire and water damage in his book.[4]

Stacks—This represents a very expensive part of the equipment to be purchased, so careful selection is particularly important. The first question to decide is the amount of shelving, based on the expected collection size to be shelved, as well as the types needed for various sizes and/or sorts of materials. For example, newspapers, current periodicals, technical reports, and regular size books all require different widths and styles of shelves for best results.

The next question concerns whether to get wood or metal shelving. The final choice may depend upon whether one is thinking of a row of shelving for reference books in a prominent part of the library, which might call for an attractive wood range, or a large stack area not prominently in view, where the efficient use of space might call for metal. A third type is mechanized shelving, which can be compacted by electromechanical devices and spread apart for readers upon receiving a signal. One system is computer-controlled, with automatic retrieval and reshelving.

In making rough estimates of the capacity of shelving, most authorities suggest a figure of 250 volumes of monographs per double-faced section three feet long, or 180-210 volumes of bound periodicals for a similar section. Another way of looking at it is the average figure of ten to fifteen volumes per square foot using normal aisles. By contrast, in a storage area closed to the public, using 102'' high shelving (versus the normal 90'' height) and shelving items by size, I was able to achieve thirty-seven volumes per square foot. However, this method would be applicable only to a closed storage area; it is entirely unsuited for public access.

Seating—Once again the question arises as to the choice between wood and metal. Although wood has been more common in university circles, the librarian should be open-minded about the matter. Most new libraries choose upholstered seats as a matter of course; users should appreciate this choice, especially if they have been accustomed to bare surface seats for any length of time.

It is most desirable to choose a standard design rather than to have a custom-made chair, simply because of the expense involved. Whatever chairs are picked, they should be considered carefully in regard to the tables or carrels to insure correct relative heights. If arm chairs are selected, the arms must slide under the table tops. Chairs that cannot easily be tipped back by casual readers will last longer.

A durable yet colorful material should be selected for the chair coverings; materials that become sticky or uncomfortable in hot weather should be avoided.

A plan providing for a few lounge chairs grouped informally near current periodicals is popular with readers. Chairs for staff members should be designed for office work, as far as back support, rollers, and height adjustability are concerned. The professional staff should have chairs appropriate to the areas and desks at which they are to be located.

Tables and Carrels—As mentioned previously, more and more libraries are finding that users prefer small tables and carrels to tables accommodating several chairs. Privacy is the end sought, and in libraries where there are individual carrels as well as multichair tables readers generally search for a carrel first before settling for a table where others may be seated.

Metal versus wood is a point to consider here also, although wood has long been a favorite in collegiate libraries.

Height in relationship to chairs is important, especially if different manufacturers are chosen for tables than for chairs. The choice of a top is affected by the possibilities of glare; hence a surface that is restful to the eyes should be selected.

Some carrels should be equipped with electric outlets for use with audiovisual aids. Carrels can be purchased in a variety of forms, some of which are quite economical of space, with up to four reading positions (each invisible to the other) possible with one type of four-sided carrel unit.

A useful estimate on the average percentages of carrels, tables, and study rooms needed for academic libraries is found in Ellsworth's text on library planning.[5] The group study rooms mentioned there are of the same type as the room described here previously in which a completely closed area is provided for in order to prevent conversations from bothering other readers. Placing typewriters in such rooms (if there is no other appropriate place for them within the library) is better than having users typing in areas where they bother many other patrons.

Filing Cabinets—Most libraries need a number of regular-sized cabinets for filing correspondence, records, and the like. Those libraries with microforms and audiovisual aids will need specially constructed cabinets designed to fit the material being stored. It is interesting to note that an eight-drawer cabinet of the sort normally designed for microfiche holds so many fiche that it provides a storage density of over six thousand fiche per square foot, a far cry from the average for books of around ten to fifteen per square foot.

If there is no storage closet, a double door cabinet is useful for library supplies. Such a cabinet for staff members' coats may be necessary if a built-in coat closet is not feasible.

Some libraries with enough file materials to justify the high costs may want to get mechanized files that provide for push-button selection and automatic retrieval of the drawer desired. Business records, journalistic clippings, and similar collections are those best suited to these types of files. Floor loadings are particularly sensitive in installations of this equipment because such files are unusually heavy.

Floor Coverings—For decades the only type of floor coverings considered for the usual sci-tech library, aside from a few with the elegance of marble, was a tile floor, made up of separately placed squares of linoleum, vinyl, or similar material. Then experiments showed that overall costs for carpets, especially when maintenance was considered, were competitive with tile floors. Of course, meaningful cost comparisons depend largely upon the amount of care given the tiles. There is no doubt, however, that carpeting is more attractive, more comfortable to walk on, and reduces noise. (For a good discussion of this subject, see

Metcalf.[6]) If carpeting is chosen, careful thought should be given to its color and design. A solid color will show soil much more than one with mottled colors, such as a tweed, preferably one with a tightly woven fabric.

Color Selection—The average university building has masonry walls, painted in solid colors. Paneled walls are a thing of the past for any but the most elegant, expensive library. Therefore, it is imperative that the paint color be carefully selected. While much has been written on this topic, it is still a subjective matter. Probably more library walls are painted off-white or a cream color than any other. In such cases, color contrast can be found in the choice of draperies (if required), floor coverings, and/or upholstery for chairs. Even painting the end panels of stacks, for example, using a variety of well-selected colors, can add effectively to the beauty of a library. Interior designers should be hired to select furniture and colors. A good treatment of this subject is found in the chapter by Mary Nikas in the collection published by the Special Libraries Association.[7]

Microform Readers and Printers—Equipment for reading and/or printing microforms cannot be quickly described in a few sentences, other than to say that the field changes quickly from year to year as new manufacturers appear, printing processes change, and innovative design features seem to proliferate with each new model. Something as relatively staid as the design and construction of shelving seems very prosaic compared to the developments in the microform equipment field. Just the selection of a reader for fiche or film can involve many factors, as shown by the checklist compiled by Loretta Kiersky in the SLA publication.[8] Printers are even more complicated, with processes varying from dry systems to those requiring chemicals in a wet process. Prices for readers and reader/printers vary tremendously, depending upon the size, versatility, and quality of the equipment. The librarian making a selection is urged to shop carefully before making a decision.

Other Special Equipment—Just as complicated is the selection of special devices, such as audiovisual equipment, computer terminals, and security systems. Again, one should get a wide view of what is available before purchases are made.

Another type of equipment finding its way into many sci-tech libraries is the desk calculator. Some universities discourage them, while others take the opposite viewpoint. The trend seems to be for their acceptance. Any library equipped with calculators of any sort must take proper security precautions, including placing them in a prominent position and fastening them securely to stationary tables. They are usually very popular with students, and sometimes the library staff also finds them helpful.

Metcalf has compiled a very useful list of equipment that might be overlooked in planning a library.[9] It ranges from wall clocks to pencil sharpeners, from drinking fountains to public telephones, and from book return slots to bulletin boards. It would be advisable to read his chapter before considering a library plan completed.

Planning Literature

Some good texts are available on planning. This is not surprising considering the importance and expense of planning and equipping libraries. A few of the books most pertinent to university and sci-tech libraries will be described here.

By far the best if Keyes Metcalf's *Planning Academic and Research Library Buildings.*[10] With its thorough treatment it is truly an indispensable reference book. The first half of the book is concerned with the nature of libraries (shelving, traffic problems, lighting, seating). The second half is devoted to the planning process, ranging from the selection of consultants up to and including construction and moving in. It is profusely illustrated with drawings and sample layouts and also has many tables.

Ralph Ellsworth, himself a noted library building consultant, has recently written a book devoted to academic library buildings.[11] His emphasis is on the process of writing a library program and on the role of consultants and architects. The chapter on formulas and space standards gathers many useful facts into one place. The book also contains many photographs.

A useful collection of articles on all aspects of university library buildings was edited by David Weber.[12] Besides the helpful article by Mason on lighting and mechanical equipment previously mentioned, there is one by Robert Walsh on branch library planning.

A publication of the Special Libraries Association, edited by the author, covers the planning and equipping processes from preplanning through moving techniques.[13] It includes an annotated bibliography, two checklists on planning (including useful formulas and standards), sample layouts for special libraries, and a selective directory of equipment manufacturers.

One of the December issues of *Library Journal* has for years contained a survey of new library construction, thus providing a useful way to keep abreast of the field. In recent years it has been compiled by Jerrold Orne.[14]

As can be seen by a reading of pertinent literature, there are many, many details in the successful planning of a library, even on just upgrading and modernizing one. Yet the planner must also keep clearly in mind the broad picture of what the objectives are, to avoid making big mistakes while catching small ones. It is a challenging experience.

Notes

[1]Keyes Metcalf, *Planning Academic and Research Library Buildings* (New York: McGraw-Hill, 1965), 431 p.

[2]Ellis Mount, ed., *Planning the Special Library* (New York: Special Libraries Association, 1972), 122 p. (SLA Monograph No. 4)

[3]David C. Weber, ed., "University Library Buildings," *Library Trends* 18, no. 2 (October 1969): 151.

[4]Metcalf, *Planning Academic*, p. 215-220.

[5]Ralph E. Ellsworth, *Planning Manual for Academic Buildings* (Metuchen, N.J.: Scarecrow Press, 1973), 159 p.

[6]Metcalf, *Planning Academic*, p. 211-213.

[7]Mount, *Planning the Special Library.*

[8]Ibid.

[9]Metcalf, *Planning Academic.*

[10]Ibid.

[11]Ellsworth, *Planning Manual.*

[12]Weber, "University Library Buildings."

[13]Mount, *Planning the Special Library.*

[14]Jerrold Orne, "Academic Library Building in 1973," *Library Journal* 98, no. 21 (December 1, 1973): 3511-3516.

10

Scientific and Engineering Literature

The subject of this chapter is extremely important since it deals with the literature and related nonprint materials that make up the sci-tech collections. The plan is to discuss the characteristics of the various types of literature and materials, such as patents, handbooks, dictionaries, and indexing services, then to list typical examples of each type. It should be apparent that in a single chapter, covering all sciences and engineering, the examples will have to be very selective. Exclusion of a title does not mean it is not first rate, nor are the examples appearing here all necessarily to be considered the very best in their class. They are merely representative of their type. For several reasons, examples will be primarily concerned with English-language works.

Working with scientists and engineers of all levels of education and experience has revealed that many of them are quite ignorant not only of certain specific major reference works but also of some entire classes of literature. More than one engineer, for example, has been found to be literally unaware that indexing and abstracting services for engineering journals even existed. So one should not assume they know a great deal about various types of literature, or how to use them, or which to use for certain purposes.

Little stress will be placed upon tools with which the average librarian, of whatever academic or work background, should be familiar. Works which go into greater depth than this chapter in describing technical and scientific literature will be cited here. (See section which follows.)

Basic Reference Works

Guides to the Literature

One of the most fundamental reference tools is the guide to the literature of a particular discipline or a group of disciplines. Such works describe the types of literature available, give examples, usually with annotations of some sort, and often evaluate the contents or compare one work cited therein with another. Another feature in such works is guidance in the use of libraries and information centers. While such guidance is of no great value to the librarian or the experienced library user, it does assist those unacquainted with the techniques of using technical collections. But librarians who are not familiar with all the major reference works in a field should use literature guides to learn about these tools, particularly early in their experience with a new subject. Doing reference work is extremely difficult if at least the major tools available are not known.

One drawback to these guides is the fact that, like any work issued without supplements, they soon get out of date. This does not mean that guides then become worthless, since the major reference works usually remain important for many years. It does mean that one must not use the guides and assume that they include all that exists, ignoring the appearance of new tools each year. By keeping abreast of what is being published as it appears, perhaps keeping a small card file as a personal reminder of very important new works, reference librarians can cope with the problem of aging reference works.

Some guides cover as broad a scope as all of science and engineering in one book. (It can be seen that the scope of this chapter is also that broad. Consequently, the treatment of all sci-tech literature in one chapter will necessarily have to be on a very narrow scale compared to the depth of coverage possible in a book on the subject.) Other guides may be devoted to two or three disciplines, such as physics and mathematics. Still others concentrate on just one subject, e.g., chemistry.

Some examples of the various kinds of literature guides available are shown below.

Science-Technology (General)

Grogan, Dennis. *Science and Technology: An Introduction to the Literature.* 2nd ed. rev. Hamden, Conn.: Shoe String, 1973. 254 p.

Offers a thorough treatment of the literature, arranged by types (patents, handbooks, etc.). An evaluation of each item is cited in a running commentary rather than in formal citation form. Thousands of examples. A careful, detailed work.

Houghton, Bernard. *Technical Information Sources: A Guide to the Patent Specifications, Standards and Technical Reports Literature.* 2d ed. Hamden, Conn.: Shoe String, 1972. 119 p.

Discusses the organization of patent systems in various countries, including the official and unofficial means of retrieving them. Sources of standards are cited. Problems of handling and retrieving technical reports are cited. Has an author and title index.

Lasworth, Earl James. *Reference Sources in Science and Technology.* Metuchen, N.J.: Scarecrow, 1972. 305 p.

Discusses the characteristics of different types of technical and scientific literature (such as handbooks, encyclopedias, translations, and periodicals), then lists selected samples, without annotations. One chapter discusses the proper style of bibliographic references, while another is on the use of a card catalog.

Malinowsky, H. Robert. *Science and Engineering Reference Sources: A Guide for Students and Librarians.* 2d ed. Littleton, Colo.: Libraries Unlimited, 1975. 400(?) p.

Provides a separate chapter for the literature of many disciplines (physics, chemistry, medicine, engineering, biology, geology, mathematics, and general science). Lists many examples, most of which are annotated. Has an author-title index.

Parke, Nathan Grier, III. *Guide to the Literature of Mathematics and*

Physics, Including Related Works on Engineering Science. 2d rev.
ed. New York: Dover, 1958. 436 p.

A comprehensive work, although in need of revision. Part I
discusses general topics (such as study habits, literature searching,
and description of types of reference books). Part II lists thousands
of texts for both specific topics (such as conformal mapping,
piezoelectricity), as well as types of literature (periodicals,
dictionaries).

Walford, A. J. *Guide to Reference Material.* Volume 1—*Science and
Technology.* 3d ed. New York: Bowker, 1973. 624 p.

Cites several thousand books and reference sources. They are
arranged into broad categories such as geology, engineering, and
chemical industry, as well as general technical works. All items are
annotated. Has an author-title index.

Astronautics

Fry, Bernard M.; F. E. Mohrhardt, eds. *A Guide to Information Sources
in Space Science and Technology.* New York: Wiley, 1963. 579 p.

Cites thousands of technical reports and periodical articles as well
as traditional reference books. Subjects covered range from
metallurgy to propulsion and astronomy. Annotations are provided
for all items. Title, author, and subject index given.

Atomic Energy

Anthony, L. J. *Sources of Information on Atomic Energy.* Elmsford,
N.Y.: Pergamon, 1966. 245 p.

For each national source of data on this topic, lists its name,
arranged by country, as well as sources on an international basis.
Chapters on published literature are then presented, selected to
cover five aspects of atomic energy, including high energy physics
and radiation.

Biology

Bottle, R. T.; H. V. Wyatt, eds. *The Use of Biological Literature.*
Hamden, Conn.: Archon Books, 1966. 286 p.

A collection of articles dealing with various types of literature
(bibliographies, journals, translations) as well as with the literature
of different aspects of biology, such as zoology, microbiology, or
agriculture. Uses a prose format to list thousands of titles, with most
of them annotated or otherwise described. Has a subject index which
also includes a few serial titles.

Chemical Engineering

Smith, Julian F.; T. E. Singer, eds. *Literature of Chemical Technology.*
Columbus, Ohio: American Chemical Society, 1968. 723 p.
(Advances in Chemistry Series No. 78)

Forty chapters discuss various aspects of the literature, such as the
literature of refractories, of the cosmetic industry, of carbon black,
of resins and plastics, etc. A thorough work, listing thousands of
literature citations. Based on two ACS Symposia held in 1963.

Chemistry

Bottle, R. T., ed. *The Use of Chemical Literature.* 2d ed. Hamden,
Conn.: Archon Books, 1969. 294 p.

A thorough listing of literature, arranged either in chapters on
types of literature (e.g., abstracting services or dictionaries) or by
subject (e.g., nuclear chemistry or inorganic chemistry). Two
chapters discuss the use of libraries and search techniques.

Mellon, M. G. *Chemical Publications: Their Nature and Use.* 4th ed.
New York: McGraw-Hill, 1965. 324 p.

An older work that is still useful. It not only gives the
characteristics of many types of literature, with examples, but also

has a lengthy chapter on the techniques of searching the chemical literature.

Earth Sciences

Wood, D. N., ed. *Use of Earth Sciences Literature.* Hamden, Conn.: Archon Books, 1974. 459 p.

Besides chapters on using the literature and on various types of literature (primary sources, secondary sources, etc.), contains chapters devoted to specific areas of study, such as mineralogy, geophysics, or paleontology. Prose accounts discuss the merits of the items cited. Lists thousands of titles.

Electrical Engineering

Burkett, Jack; P. Plumb. *How to Find Out in Electrical Engineering.* Elmsford, N.Y.: Pergamon, 1967. 234 p.

Arranged by the Universal Decimal Classification for the arrangement of sources, with chapters devoted to such subjects as electronics, power generation, and data processing. Chapters are given on such forms of literature as encyclopedias, tables, and periodicals.

Engineering (General)

Mount, Ellis. *Guide to Basic Information Sources in Engineering.* New York: Jeffrey Norton, in prep.

Presents chapters on the use of libraries and search techniques, while other chapters center on specific forms of literature, ranging from bibliographies to maps, or from patents to trade catalogs. All items are annotated.

Parsons, Stanley Alfred James. *How to Find Out about Engineering.* New York: Pergamon, 1972. 271 p.

Early chapters cover such topics as engineering careers and the use of libraries, followed by chapters on various types of materials (handbooks, periodicals, etc.) Other chapters cover specific branches of engineering (e.g., electrical, civil, mining). Selected examples of literature are described. Has name and subject (plus title) indexes.

History of Science

Sarton, George. *A Guide to the History of Science: A First Guide for the Study of the History of Science with Introductory Essays on Science and Tradition.* New York: Ronald, 1952. 316 p.

Essentially a detailed guide to the literature, with some chapters concerned with different types of literature and others arranged by the country studied or by specific topics, such as optics or zoology. Has an index of personal names.

Mathematics

Pemberton, John E. *How to Find Out in Mathematics: A Guide to Sources of Information.* 2d rev. ed. New York: Pergamon, 1969. 193 p.

Besides emphasis on the specific types of literature, contains chapters devoted to discussions of mathematical societies, literature on operations research and probability, as well as Russian literature. Has an author index. Most items are annotated or otherwise described.

Mechanical Engineering

Houghton, Bernard. *Mechanical Engineering: The Sources of Information.* Hamden, Conn.: Shoe String, 1970. 311 p.

A comprehensive guide that covers not only the different types of literature but also describes other sources of information, such as government agencies, trade associations, and research institutions. Cites hundreds of examples, most of which are not annotated. Has an author-title index.

Metals and Metallurgical Engineering

Gibson, Eleanor B.; E. W. Tapia, eds. *Guide to Metallurgical Information.* 2d ed. New York: Special Libraries Association, 1965. 222 p. (SLA Bibliography no. 3)

Cites types of literature of interest to metallurgists and lists pertinent information centers. All cited items are annotated. Provides several indexes, including personal authors, subjects, titles, and organization names.

Hyslop, Marjorie R. *A Brief Guide to Sources of Metals Information.* Washington, D. C.: Information Resources Press, 1974. 180 p.

The author's familiarity with this topic makes this of special value. Besides instruction in the use of libraries, it gives descriptions of the many types of literature of interest to metallurgists. Includes a directory of information sources plus a chapter on the setting up of personal information systems.

Mining Engineering and Minerals

Kaplan, Stuart R., ed. *Guide to Information Sources in Mining, Minerals and Geosciences.* New York: Wiley, 1965. 599 p.

The first part lists important source organizations on a geographical basis, indicating fields of study, publications, etc. The second part lists major types of literature for each of twenty disciplines, such as geology, mining, and physics.

Physics

Whitford, Robert N. *Physics Literature: A Reference Manual.* 2d ed. Metuchen, N.J.: Scarecrow, 1968. 272 p.

Organized according to type of physics literature, such as historical, biographical, and mathematical. Cites thousands of examples, giving concise comments for many of them. Has an author and subject index.

Yates, Bryan. *How to Find Out about Physics: A Guide to Sources of Information.* Elmsford, N.Y.: Pergamon, 1965. 175 p.

> Presents sources of information arranged by the decimal system, with chapters dealing with such broad headings as optics, atomic physics, or heat. Some chapters discuss types of literature (periodicals, documents). The index is selective, listing only certain titles and subjects.

Psychology

White, Carl M. and others. *Sources of Information in the Social Sciences: A Guide to the Literature.* 2d ed. Chicago: American Library Association, 1973. 702 p.

> One of the nine parts is devoted to psychology, consisting of fifty pages. Part of the material is arranged by subject (e.g., applied psychology or perception) and part is organized by type of literature. Items are mostly annotated. Lists nearly five hundred items.

Bibliographies

Current—As any librarian knows, there are long-established indexes to current and in-print monographs, such as *Books in Print* and *Cumulative Book Index.* These works are indispensable for general purposes, whether it be for checking citations, searching for a particular work, or selecting new materials for purchase. Being national in scope, reliable, and reasonable in price, they are usually available in sci-tech libraries of all sorts. However, there are also important, broad-based serial publications which are devoted to science and engineering.

One special version of *Books in Print* which began in recent years is the following:

Scientific and Technical Books in Print. New York: Bowker, 1972-   . Annual.

> Provides indexes by author, title, and subject for selected engineering and scientific monographs, chosen from the overall

Books in Print data base. Serves to concentrate attention on the books apt to interest sci-tech libraries. Covers more than 57,000 books.

For those seeking information on selected new books, restricted to titles which are scientific and technical, these two well-known indexes are recommended:

New Technical Books. New York: New York Public Library, Research
     Libraries, 1915-   . Ten issues per years.

> An annotated listing of new monographs recently added to the collection of this library. Each issue has an author and a subject index, which cumulate annually. Presents a broad selection of titles, but primarily restricted to those in English.

Technical Book Review Index. Pittsburgh: Special Libraries Associa-
     tion, 1935-   . Ten issues per year.

> Presents a selection of book reviews of technical and scientific books. Sometimes more than one review is cited. Helps in selection of borderline books, when a choice is not obvious from the title or other criteria. Has an annual author index.

Other means of keeping abreast of new sci-tech books include, of course, publishers' advertisements, accession lists of sci-tech libraries willing to furnish copies, and reviews of books in various trade and professional journals.

Bibliographies—Retrospective

A bibliography can be devoted to a relatively broad subject or to a very narrow one. In this section both types will be discussed, showing their features as compared to the broader scope of the works discussed in the previous section. A broad subject might be exemplified by electronics, or computers, or even science in general. A specific subject, on the other hand, might be a work devoted to a narrow topic like airport noise.

Special bibliographies, unlike the current publications listed in the previous section, are rarely updated more frequently than on an annual basis, and most are issued only as single publications without further updating. Thus, they are more useful for retrospective searching or for building up neglected collections than for keeping one aware of current titles, which they do not pretend to try to do.

There are many ways of organizing bibliographies, some being more useful than others. Many librarians favor those arranged by broad subject categories, with a detailed subject index at the end of the work, along with an author index. Arrangement within the broad classes might be by author. Then there are those bibliographies arranged by specific subjects, with author indexes and cross references for related subjects. Two other types are those arranged by author or chronologically by date of publication, with supplementary subject and author indexes, as needed. The latter two have less value than the first two. Some have annotations, or abstracts, and some do not. Obviously, bibliographies with annotations are much more useful than those without.

The biggest drawback to bibliographies is that, like literature guides, they get out of date quickly. However, they are indispensable to a search of older literature. Once this has been done, the searcher has only to check the more recent literature, thus usually saving considerable time. Another problem is to find a bibliography exactly on the topic one is searching. There are not great quantities of bibliographies, especially in book form, so one may have to go to the periodical or technical report literature to find bibliographies on the specific topic desired.

Although this section will be restricted to examples from the book literature, the examples of bibliographies found in periodicals or reports which would have been cited would be similar except that they would probably be narrower in scope. Size, for one thing, would prohibit a journal editor from accepting a huge bibliography on a broad subject for publication, whereas it might be appropriate for publication as a book. In fact, it might have more chance of acceptance as a book if it covered a rather broad subject, since the potential audience for it would be correspondingly larger.

Science and Engineering (General)

Jenkins, Frances B. *Science Reference Sources.* 5th ed. Cambridge, Mass.: MIT Press, 1969. 231 p.

A bibliography arranged by type of literature under the broad categories of science (mathematics, physics, chemistry, astronomy, earth sciences, biological sciences, medical sciences, agricultural sciences) and engineering. There are no annotations, but an author-title index is provided.

Lunsford, Effie B.; Theodore J. Kopin. *A Basic Collection for Scientific and Technical Libraries.* New York: Special Libraries Association, 1971. 274 p.

Lists twenty-four hundred items in classed order, with author and serial indexes. There are brief annotations.

McGraw-Hill Basic Bibliography of Science and Technology. Edited by T. C. Hines. New York: McGraw-Hill, 1966. 738 p.

Over seven thousand technical and scientific terms are related to one or more references from the literature, with brief annotations. Has an alphabetical arrangement, with a classed index in an appendix.

Astronomy

Kemp, D. A. *Astronomy and Astrophysics: A Bibliographical Guide.* Hamden, Conn.: Shoe String, 1970. 584 p.

Lists sources of information (reference works, journal articles, etc.) with annotations. Then follows an annotated bibliography of specific articles and books arranged by broad subject categories. There is a detailed subject index and an author index.

Earth Sciences

Ward, Dederick C. and others. *Geologic Reference Sources: A Subject and Regional Bibliography of Publications and Maps in the Geological Sciences.* Metuchen, N.J.: Scarecrow, 1972. 453 p.

A bibliography arranged in four sections: general, subject, regional, and maps. Has occasional annotations. There are geographical and subject indexes.

Environmental Studies

Winton, Harry N. M. *Man and the Environment: A Bibliography of Selected Publications of the United Nations System, 1946-1971.* New York: Unipub, 1972. 305 p.

Arranged in broad subject classes. Has indexes for authors, titles, subjects, and serials/series numbers. Covers a wide range of topics. Has around twelve hundred items, mostly annotated.

Psychology

Harvard University. *The Harvard List of Books in Psychology.* Compiled and annotated by the psychologists in Harvard University. 4th ed. Cambridge, Mass.: Harvard University Press, 1971. 108 p.

An annotated bibliography of selected titles in the main branches of psychology. There are short annotations plus an author index.

Encyclopedias

Librarians know, as uninformed library users may not, that there are many types of encyclopedias besides the general works commonly found in the home, public libraries, or school libraries. While even these have their degrees of quality and depth of scholarship in preparation, this section is devoted to encyclopedias of a scientific and/or technical nature. The scope of coverage may range from a one-volume work covering all of the sciences, to a multivolume set covering analytical chemistry. Some bear the name "encyclopedia" in their titles, and some do not. The main identifying features are that they are usually written by teams of specialists, with articles usually in alphabetical order, which range from a portion of a column to several pages; literature references usually abound.

Some of the sets have irregularly issued supplements, while a few have annual yearbooks. Others have no supplements, which limits their usefulness after a certain number of years. Age, however, does not affect them as much when the topics are largely theoretical and basic as when they are devoted to current types of hardware and techniques. The convenience of having all the important topics on a given subject in one work or one set of volumes is a great asset.

The examples given here will include all types of encyclopedias, both narrow subjects and broad ones, single volumes and multivolume sets.

Science and Engineering (General)

Harper Encyclopedia of Science. Rev. ed. Edited by James R. Newman. New York: Harper & Row, 1967. 1,379 p.

> Includes all areas of science and engineering, with articles ranging from a few lines to several pages in length. Profusely illustrated with photographs, drawings, charts, many in color. A useful quick source to use for a first look at a topic.

McGraw-Hill Encyclopedia of Science and Technology. 3d ed. New York: McGraw-Hill, 1971- . 15 vols. and annual supplements.

> Widely acknowledged as a very useful set (over ten thousand pages in length), covering science and technology comprehensively. Very well-edited and -illustrated. Has signed articles, many being several pages in length. Has a separate index volume. Updated by *McGraw-Hill Yearbook of Science and Technology* (which see). Also a separate readers' guide and a study guide are available, to aid the user.

Van Nostrand's Scientific Encyclopedia. 4th ed. New York: Van Nostrand Reinhold, 1968. 2,008 p.

> Covers all aspects of science and engineering, there being around 16,500 articles, well-illustrated, many in color. Articles range from a brief statement to several pages.

Astronautics

McGraw-Hill Encyclopedia of Space. New York: McGraw-Hill, 1968. 831 p.

Profusely illustrated, often in color. Text deals with rockets, satellites, space navigation, man in space, astrophysics, moon travel, and related aspects of space exploration.

Astronomy

Flamarrion, Gabrielle Camille; André Donjon. *The Flamarrion Book of Astronomy*. New York: Simon and Schuster, 1964. 670 p.

A translation of the French edition. Has major sections devoted to each topic, e.g., the earth, moon, sun, planets, instruments, and space exploration. Well-illustrated.

Biology

Gray, Peter, ed. *Encyclopedia of the Biological Sciences*. 2d ed. New York: Van Nostrand Reinhold, 1970. 1,027 p.

Has around eight hundred signed articles, most several pages in length, covering all aspects of biology, excluding applied biological sciences. Has a detailed subject index.

Chemical Engineering

Encyclopedia of Chemical Technology. 2d ed. Edited by R. E. Kirk and D. F. Othmer. New York: Wiley, 1963- .

Presents an outstanding treatment of the subject, totaling twenty-two volumes. About half the articles, which are signed, deal with chemical substances, while there are also articles on industrial processes and fundamental topics. Very thorough. Supplements are issued irregularly.

Encyclopedia of Industrial Chemical Analysis. Edited by Foster O. Snell and others. New York: Wiley, 1966-1974. 20 vols.

Articles range from a few lines to many pages in length. Well-illustrated, with many cross-references.

Chemistry

Hampel, Clifford; G. G. Hawley, eds. *Encyclopedia of Chemistry.* 3d ed. New York: Van Nostrand Reinhold, 1973. 1,216 p.

Discusses virtually every aspect of advances in chemistry since 1966. Contains more than five hundred articles, and any material that was retained from the previous edition has been completely updated.

Earth Sciences

Fairbridge, Rhodes W., ed. *Encyclopedia of Earth Sciences.* New York: Van Nostrand Reinhold, 1966-   . Issued irregularly.

A series of works dealing, in separate volumes, with such topics as oceanography, atmospheric sciences, geomorphology, and geochemistry. Articles are generally thorough, with adequate references to the literature. Four volumes had been published by 1974.

Environmental Studies

McGraw-Hill Encyclopedia of Environmental Science. New York: McGraw-Hill, 1974. 700 p.

Contains 300 articles, well-illustrated, involving such areas as meteorology, ecology, conservation, oceanography, soils, mining, and civil engineering in relation to the environment.

Minerals

Encyclopedia of Minerals. Edited by Willard Lincoln Roberts and others. New York: Van Nostrand Reinhold, 1974. 848p.

Provides chemical, physical, crystallographic, x-ray, optical, and geographical data on more than 200 minerals. Includes nearly one thousand full-color photographs.

Physics

Encyclopaedic Dictionary of Physics. Edited by J. Thewlis. Elmsford, N.Y.: Pergamon, 1961-

Consists of rather detailed signed articles on all aspects of physics as well as some coverage of topics in mathematics, astronomy, physical metallurgy, physical chemistry, etc., covering nine volumes. Volume eight contains subject and author indexes. Volume nine is a six-language multilingual dictionary. Supplements have been issued every two years or so, totaling four by 1974.

Handbuch der Physik. Encyclopedia of Physics. Berlin: Springer, 1955- . Issued irregularly.

By 1974 over seventy volumes had been published in this set, with each volume devoted to a topic such as fluid dynamics, magnetism, or acoustics. Some topics require more than one volume to complete them.

Safety

International Labour Organization. *Encyclopedia of Occupational Health and Safety.* New York, McGraw-Hill, 1972. 1,600 p.

Takes into account the most recent developments in industry, medicine, and accident prevention. Its concise articles cover a wide range of topics in this field. Has ample cross-references.

Dictionaries

Scientific and technical dictionaries, like the literature already discussed, can range from those works encompassing many disciplines to those restricted to one small subject area. Another distinct feature of dictionaries is that some are entirely in one language, while others are bilingual or multilingual. Those entirely in one language may have very lengthy definitions, including graphs, illustrations, and chemical structures. On the other hand, the definitions may be barely adequate. It is often difficult for the compiler to limit terms to just one discipline, so that a dictionary on physics, for example, may well include many terms from chemistry, mathematics, and related fields. Others can be more specific, so that a dictionary on computers may be very strict in excluding terms from fringe subject areas.

The need for foreign-language dictionaries is great for the scientist or engineer who is not content with English-language works, yet who needs to translate an item without the delay and/or expense of having a translator do it. Americans have traditionally been so poor at linguistics that they seem to need more and more help in using foreign-language material. The multilingual dictionaries have one advantage: they offer several languages in one volume at a price lower than that of a separate volume for each language involved. However, multilingual dictionaries rarely give substantial definitions. Instead they usually give only the equivalent term in other languages. It is common for such works to have an alphabetical index for each language involved in the work, normally at the back of the volume, with a reference to the page in which other foreign equivalents are to be found for each term. Arrangement of terms is usually alphabetical by the main language, which is usually English in Western publications.

Bilingual dictionaries are sometimes limited to a one-way translation of terms, such as German to English. Others are on a two-way basis, e.g., both German to English and English to German. In English-speaking countries it is obviously more important to have the foreign language-to-English arrangement. Probably only if a person were trying to translate English into a foreign language would the need for English-to-foreign language be apt to arise. Most libraries, except for those with very strong collections, do not seek out bilingual technical dictionaries if neither language is English. If they do collect them, they may be relegated to the regular stacks, not the reference shelf, as a work involving English would be treated. Definitions in bilingual dictionaries are rarely detailed, tending to be on the brief side.

In view of the many scientific and technical topics suitable for dictionaries, as well as the many languages of the world, one can see that the theoretical total combinations of subjects and languages is almost limitless. It is conceivable that an Icelandic-Rumanian dictionary on welding might be compiled, likewise a Spanish-Turkish dictionary on botany. Or by adding other languages to these two works, making them multilingual, many other possibilities could be devised. Such works are unlikely to be published because there would be little demand for them. Unless a work includes one or more of the dominant languages of technical publications, interest will be slight. For example, an English-Icelandic dictionary on welding might be of sufficient interest to engineers and technicians in Iceland to make it worthwhile, in view of the vast amount of scientific and technical literature in English on this subject. But such a work would be of little interest in the United States.

While it is difficult to rate popularity of languages, most sci-tech libraries in universities in America find the demand for foreign-language dictionaries to be heaviest for those involving German, French, and Russian. This does not imply that dictionaries in other languages are not requested, but merely that these three seem to be the most commonly used tongues.

English Language—Science and Engineering (General)

Ballentyne, D.W.G., ed. *A Dictionary of Named Effects and Laws in Chemistry, Physics and Mathematics.* 3d ed. New York: Barnes & Noble, 1970. 205 p.

> Consists of an alphabetical listing under the name of the one for whom the law or effect is named. Includes mathematical expressions, where necessary, for clarity.

McGraw-Hill Dictionary of Scientific and Technical Terms. Edited by Daniel N. Lapedes. New York: McGraw-Hill, 1974. 1,634 p.

> Has almost one hundred thousand concise definitions from all fields of science and technology, as well as over three thousand photographs, drawings, and other illustrations.

English Language—Abbreviations, Symbols, Etc.

De Sola, Ralph. *Abbreviations Dictionary.* 4th ed. New York: American Elsevier, 1974. 428 p.

> Presents more than one hundred thirty thousand definitions and entries. Includes abbreviations, anonyms, acronyms, contractions, initials, and nicknames.

Polon, David D. *DPMA: Dictionary of Physics and Mathematics Abbreviations, Signs and Symbols.* New York: Technical Library Service, 1965. 333 p.

> Includes abbreviations, letter symbols, mathematical signs and symbols, abbreviations for learned societies and government agencies, plus related tables. Many tables are also listed in reverse order, to facilitate their use.

English Language—Aerospace Science

Gentle, Ernest J.; Lawrence W. Reithmaier, eds. *Aviation and Space Dictionary.* 5th ed. Fallbrook, Calif.: Aero, 1974. 272 p.

> Includes terms not only for aerospace subjects but also for such fields as geophysics, nucleonics, and computer technology.

English Language—Biology

Gray, Peter, comp. *The Dictionary of the Biological Sciences.* New York: Van Nostrand Reinhold, 1967. 602 p.

> Contains over forty thousand entries, consisting of words in general use among biologists. Has brief definitions.

English Language—Chemistry

Condensed Chemical Dictionary. 8th ed. Edited by Gessner G. Hawley. New York: Van Nostrand Reinhold, 1971. 971 p.

> Indexes eighteen thousand entries. Gives name, formula, specific properties of chemicals, source, derivation, hazards involved, uses, and shipping regulations. There is also an index of manufacturers of products having a trademark.

English Language—Civil Engineering

Vollmer, Ernst, comp. *Encyclopedia of Hydraulics, Soil and Foundation Engineering.* New York: American Elsevier, 1967. 398 p.

This work could more aptly be described as a dictionary, since no entry is more than a few lines in length. Has a few drawings.

English Language—Data Processing

Condensed Computer Encyclopedia. Edited by Philip B. Jordain and Michael Breslau. New York: McGraw-Hill, 1969. 605 p.

Gives brief descriptions of technical terms and some slang expressions. Has occasional charts and drawings. Useful to many levels of users.

English Language—Electronics

Markus, John, comp. *Electronics and Nucleonics Dictionary.* 3d ed. New York: McGraw-Hill, 1967. 743 p.

Defines over sixteen thousand terms. Most definitions are several lines long. Has frequent illustrations.

English Language—Geology

Challinor, John. *Dictionary of Geology.* 4th ed. New York: Oxford University Press, 1974. 350 p.

Has carefully written definitions for fifteen hundred terms, with a citation or reference in which they are defined. There is a classified index included.

English Language—Mathematics

James, Glenn; R. C. James, comps. *Mathematics Dictionary.* 3d ed. New York: Van Nostrand Reinhold, 1968. 517 p.

The major portion consists of English terms and their definitions. In addition, there are separate indexes of terms in French, German, Russian, and Spanish, giving the English equivalents.

English Language—Mechanical Engineering

Horner, J. G., comp. *Dictionary of Mechanical Engineering Terms.* 9th ed. New York: Heinman, 1967. 422 p.

Includes terms for metallurgy, metalworking, etc., besides mechanical power terms.

English Language—Metals and Metallurgy

Osborne, A. K., comp. *An Encyclopedia of the Iron and Steel Industry.* 2d ed. New York: Heinman, 1967. 588 p.

Serves as a dictionary of terms, with the definitions averaging several lines in length. Has a wide scope, including metal-working and instruments. Includes a detailed twenty-eight page bibliography.

English Language—Mining

Nelson, A.; K. D. Nelson, eds. *Dictionary of Applied Geology: Mining and Engineering.* New York: Philosophical Library, 1967. 421 p.

Presents brief definitions for names of minerals, rock types, building materials, soils, etc. Intended primarily for those in mining and civil engineering.

English Language—Nuclear Engineering

Hughes, L. E. and others, eds. *Dictionary of Electronics and Nucleonics.* New York: Barnes and Noble, 1970. 443 p.

Offers concise definitions as well as over one hundred pages of supplementary matter, such as properties of materials used in electronics and special tables.

English Language—Physics

Thewlis, James, comp. *Concise Dictionary of Physics and Related Subjects.* New York: Pergamon, 1973. 366 p.

Gives short but adequate definitions, covering not only physics but related topics such as astronomy, geophysics, mathematics, and meteorology as well. Has many cross-references.

English Language—Psychology

Wolman, Benjamin B. *Dictionary of Behavioral Science.* New York: Van Nostrand Reinhold, 1973. 512 p.

Contains twenty thousand definitions in psychology, psychoanalysis, biochemistry, and related fields. Represents the work of nearly one hundred authorities.

Foreign Language—French

DeVries, Louis, comp. *French-English Science Dictionary: For Students in Agricultural, Biological and Physical Sciences.* 3d ed. New York: McGraw-Hill, 1962. 655 p.

Has a wide scope. Includes a revised supplement of terms in such fields as aeronautics, electronics, atomic energy, and nuclear science. There is a "Grammatical Guide for Translators" section for those needing a review of grammar.

Foreign Language—German

DeVries, Louis, comp. *German-English Science Dictionary: For Students in Chemistry, Physics, Biology, Agriculture and Related Sciences.* 3d ed., including supplement of new terms. New York: McGraw-Hill, 1959. 592 p.

Since the previous edition, over three thousand terms were added. Includes a section entitled "Suggestions for Translators," to aid the inexperienced reader of German.

Dorian, A. F., comp. *Dictionary of Science and Technology* (German-English and English-German). New York: American Elsevier, 1967, 1970. 2 vols.

The two volumes have a combined paging of over two thousand pages, making this a set of significance.

Oppermann, Alfred, comp. *Dictionary of Modern Engineering.* Volume 1 is English-German. 3d ed. 1972. Volume 2 is German-English. 1973. New York: International Publications Services, 1972-1973. 2 vols.

Offers a useful compilation of engineering terms, with German equivalents.

Foreign Language—Italian

Denti, Renzo I., comp. *Italian-English, English-Italian Technical Dictionary.* 7th ed. New York: Heinman, 1970. 1,613 p.

Covers engineering as well as pure sciences.

Foreign Language—Russian

Alford, M.H.T.; V. L. Alford, comps. *Russian-English Scientific and Technical Dictionary.* Elmsford, N.Y.: Pergamon, 1970. 2 vols.

Contains over one hundred thousand entries for ninety-four disciplines. Includes accent marks to aid pronunciation.

Foreign Language—Spanish

Sell, Lewis L., comp. *Comprehensive Technical Dictionary.* New York: McGraw-Hill, 1956, 1959. 2 vols.

Concerns all areas of engineering and technology. Volume I (in two parts) is for English to Spanish, while Volume II is for Spanish to English.

Foreign Language—Multilingual

Amstutz, G. C., comp. *Glossary of Mining Geology.* New York: American Elsevier, 1971. 196 p.

Defines terms involving mining and economic geology. Cross references are provided for the equivalent terms in Spanish, French, and German.

Biass-Ducroux, Françoise, comp. *Glossary of Genetics in English, French, Spanish, Italian, German, Russian.* New York: American Elsevier, 1970. 436 p.

Terms arranged by English words, with foreign equivalents in sequence. Has an index for each of the non-English languages. Does not define terms.

Clason, W. E., comp. *Dictionary of General Physics.* New York: American Elsevier, 1962. 859 p.

Arrranged by English terms, with definitions and foreign equivalents given. Other languages used are French, Spanish, Italian, Dutch, and German.

Clason, W. E., comp. *Dictionary of Metallurgy.* New York: American Elsevier, 1967. 634 p.

Presents terms in English (no definitions) with equivalents in French, Spanish, Italian, Dutch, and German. Each foreign language has an index of its own.

International Dictionary of Applied Mathematics. New York: Van Nostrand Reinhold, 1960. 1,173 p.

Gives definitions for the application of mathematics to thirty-one fields of physical science and engineering. Special tables give foreign terms in French, German, Russian, and Spanish and their English equivalents.

Kleczek, Josip, comp. *Astronomical Dictionary.* New York: Academic, 1962. 972 p.

> Terms are in English, Russian, German, French, Italian, and Czech. Includes some terms from related disciplines, such as mathematics and atomic physics.

Sobecka, Z. and others, eds. *Dictionary of Chemistry and Chemical Technology in Six Languages.* 2d ed. New York: Pergamon, 1966. 1,325 p.

> Consists of terms in English, German, Spanish, French, Polish, and Russian. Has no definitions, giving only foreign equivalents to the English terms.

Handbooks

There are times when a scientist or engineer may want a quick way to find a given formula, or a description of a well-known phenomenon, or details about a special piece of equipment. In many cases such queries can be promptly answered by handbooks. They abound much more in some disciplines, such as engineering, than others. They do get out of date, and, because of the great expense of publishing them, are not frequently revised. They are not inexpensive to purchase. Yet, in spite of these negative aspects, handbooks still should be considered an indispensable part of a reference collection.

They can be characterized as works with chapters written by different specialists (with a general editor for the work), with pertinent literature cited abundantly, with many tables and charts, written in a rather terse style for the sake of compactness, and with a detailed subject index (in most cases). Consequently, they are authoritative and quick to use. On the other hand, they are not written for neophytes, particularly as compared to textbooks or basic encyclopedias. Handbooks serve best the person who already has some knowledge of the basic ideas involved before the book is used. They rarely explain how formulas are derived or give much explanatory material in a tutorial style. Beginners may understand part of a description therein, but not all of it.

Their subject matter, as is the case with other types of literature, varies widely in scope and depth of treatment. A handbook on the entire subject of physics might not be much larger than one confined to a narrow topic, such as piping. One can go into much greater detail about its subject than the other. Yet both serve a useful purpose.

Biology

Keleti, Georg; William H. Lederer. *Handbook of Micromethods for the Biological Sciences.* New York: Van Nostrand Reinhold, 1973. 166 p.

> Describes over one hundred methods involving biochemical or microbiological procedures for preparation or analysis. Written in a step-by-step fashion.

Chemical Engineering

Perry, John H.; Cecil H. Chilton, eds. *Chemical Engineers' Handbook.* 5th ed. New York: McGraw-Hill, 1973. Variously paged.

> Uses over two dozen chapters to deal with basic fundamental topics (heat transfer, refrigeration, ion exchange, process control, etc.), as well as a few related subjects (electrical engineering, cost estimation, mechanical engineering, etc.).

Chemistry

Beilstein's Handbuch der organischen Chemie. 4th ed. New York: Springer-Verlag, 1918-   . Supplements issued irregularly.

> Said to be the largest compilation of information on organic chemistry. A voluminous work, with a set presently consisting of over 130 volumes, this edition has had three supplements. Gives information on compounds as to structure, preparation, history, analysis, etc. Has subject and formula indexes. Not a simple tool to use.

Civil Engineering

Merritt, Frederick S., ed. *Standard Handbook for Civil Engineers.* New York: McGraw-Hill, 1968. 1,326 p.

Topics covered include use of computers in civil engineering, specifications, construction management and materials, structural theory, foundation engineering, surveying, municipal and regional planning, as well as the engineering of highways, bridges, airports, rail transportation, tunnels, water supplies, sewage plants, harbors, etc.

Computers

Klerer, Melvin: G. A. Korn. *Digital Computer User's Handbook.* New York: McGraw-Hill, 1967. 750 p.

A work intended for computer users other than those trained in programming or numerical analysis. Section one is devoted to programming, section two to numerical techniques, section three to statistical methods, and the last section covers computer applications.

Electrical Engineering

Fink, Donald G.; J. H. Carroll, eds. *Standard Handbook for Electrical Engineers.* 10th ed. New York: McGraw-Hill, 1968. 2,300 p.

Continues the series formerly edited by A. E. Knowlton. The twenty-nine chapters discuss all aspects of the subject, such as generators, power plants (including nuclear types), motors, electronic data processing, and power transmission. Very comprehensive.

Engineering (General)

Potter, James H., ed. *Handbook of the Engineering Sciences.* New York: Van Nostrand Reinhold, 1967. 2 vols.

Volume one, on the basic sciences, discusses the basic formulas and principles of mathematics, physics, chemistry, graphics, statistics, mechanics, etc. Volume two, on the applied sciences, covers such areas as thermal phenomena, electronics, electromechanical energy conversion, astronautics, control systems, and materials science. Aimed at the first-year graduate level.

Environmental Engineering

CRC Handbook of Environmental Control. Edited by Richard G. Bond and Conrad P. Straub. Cleveland: CRC Press, 1973-1974. 4 vols.

Volume one is on air pollution, volume two covers solid waste, volume three covers water supply and treatment, while volume four is on wastewater treatment and disposal. The emphasis is on tabular data. Includes both scientific and socioeconomic factors.

Lund, Herbert F., ed. *Industrial Pollution Control Handbook.* New York: McGraw-Hill, 1971. Variously paged.

Has three main sections, with the first concerned with the basic background (history, standards, programs, etc.). The second part discusses the problems of each of eleven industrial areas (steel, paper, etc.). The last section is devoted to control equipment and its operation.

Industrial Engineering

Ireson, William Grant; Eugene L. Grant, eds. *Handbook of Industrial Engineering and Management.* 2d ed. Englewood Cliffs, N.J.: Prentice-Hall, 1970. 907 p.

A work aimed not only at industrial engineers but also at engineers now engaged in management activities. Chapters range from managerial economics to critical-path methods, from industrial safety to attitudes of labor towards industrial engineering methods, etc. Includes bibliographies.

Materials Science

CRC Handbook of Materials Science. Edited by Charles T. Lynch. Cleveland: CRC Press, 1974. 500 p.

Provides a guide, largely in tables, to properties of metals, oxides, glasses, polymers, composites, electronic materials, nuclear materials, biomedical materials, etc.

Mathematics

Hicks, Tyler G., ed. *Standard Handbook of Engineering Calculations.* New York: McGraw-Hill, 1972. Variously paged.

Presents step-by-step procedures for making more than two thousand calculations involving routine problems found in daily engineering practice. There is a separate chapter for each of twelve basic types of engineering (e.g., civil, mechanical, sanitary, chemical).

Korn, Granino; T. M. Korn. *Mathematical Handbook for Scientists and Engineers.* 2d ed. New York: McGraw-Hill, 1967. 1,130 p.

Presents a comprehensive collection of definitions, theorems, and formulas, plus some numerical tables (ranging from squares to Chebyshev polynomials). Both undergraduate and graduate subjects are included.

Mechanical Engineering

Baumeister, T.; L. Marks, eds. *Standard Handbook for Mechanical Engineers.* 7th Ed. New York: McGraw-Hill, 1967. 2,464 p.

A comprehensive work encompassing materials, mechanical properties and phenomena, mathematics, power sources, transportation, electronics, mechanisms, optics, and dozens of other subjects. Extremely useful.

Metals and Metal Working

American Society for Metals. *Metals Handbook.* 8th ed. Metals Park, Ohio, 1961- .

A monumental set of many volumes that has been under way since 1961. Volumes issued to date include: 1—Properties and selection of metals; 2—Heat treating, cleaning and finishing; 3—Machining; 4—Forming; 5—Forging and casting; 6—Welding; 7—Metallography. Additional volumes are planned.

Minerals

Hurlbut, Cornelius S., Jr. *Dana's Manual of Mineralogy.* 18th ed. New York: Wiley, 1971. 579 p.

A well-known reference source. Serves as a handbook on the properties, occurrences, and uses of around two hundred minerals. Other portions of the book discuss crystallography, physical mineralogy, chemical mineralogy, etc. Has a subject and mineral index.

Mining

SME Mining Engineering Handbook. Edited by Arthur B. Cummins and Ivan A. Given. New York: Society of Mining Engineers of AIME, 1973. 2 vols.

In thirty-five chapters deals with all aspects of mining, ranging from safety to rock mechanics, from strip mining to mineral processing. A valuable set of volumes for this field.

Nuclear Engineering

U.S. Atomic Energy Commission. *Reactor Handbook.* 2d ed. New York: Wiley, 1960-1964. 5 vols.

The set consists of: Volume 1, Materials—1960; Volume 2, Fuel reprocessing—1961; Volume 3, Pt. A, Physics—1962; Volume 3, Pt. B, Shielding—1962; Volume 4, Engineering—2d ed., 1964. As the titles indicate, all phases of the subject are covered. Stresses the materials and engineering topics more than other aspects.

Ocean Engineering and Oceanography

Myers, John J. and others, eds. *Handbook of Ocean and Underwater Engineering.* New York: McGraw-Hill, 1969. 800 p.

Discusses basic oceanography, underwater cables, fixed structures, diving, wind and wave loads, ocean operations, etc. There are twelve chapters in all.

Physics

American Institute of Physics. *Physics Handbook.* 3d ed. Edited by Dwight E. Gray. New York: McGraw-Hill, 1972. 2,220 p.

Consists of detailed treatment of large, basic topics, such as heat, nuclear physics, optics, electricity, and magnetism. Has many charts and tables.

Production

Production Handbook. 3d ed. Edited by Gordon B. Carson. New York: Ronald Press, 1972. Variously paged.

Covers a wide scope of subjects, such as purchasing, work simplification, operations research, plant layout, and plant maintenance.

Psychology

Wolman, Benjamin B., ed. *Handbook of Clinical Psychology.* New York: McGraw-Hill, 1965. 1,596 p.

In six sections deals with such topics as research methods,

diagnostic methods, and clinical patterns. Over fifty chapters take up specialized topics in each section. Has a name and subject index.

Quality Control and Reliability

Juran, J. M. *Quality Control Handbook.* 3d ed. New York: McGraw-Hill, 1974. 1,600 p.

Provides practical solutions to the quality problems encountered at all stages of production, from design to finished product. Includes costs, motivation, sampling techniques, specifications, etc.

Technical Writing

Jordan, Stello, ed. *Handbook of Technical Writing Practices.* New York: Wiley-Interscience, 1971. 2 vols.

Has thirty-two chapters dealing with diverse topics, as exemplified by equipment instruction manuals, technical reports, sales literature, and technical films. Aimed at improving the quality of technical writing, covering a wide range of users, both commercial and military.

Serials

The previous section was concerned largely with monographs, and their importance to sci-tech libraries should be evident. However, if any one type of literature could be selected as the most important type for sci-tech libraries, it would have to be serial literature. The main reason is that the constant state of progress and innovation in the sciences and engineering demands a type of literature that can report promptly, and in detail, on what these changes are. Most monographs take far too long to publish to serve this purpose. (It is not unusual for at least a year to pass between acceptance of a manuscript for a book and its completed publication.) Periodicals, on the other hand, can sometimes publish information obtained only a week or so before the publication appears.

This section will deal with the most common types of serials, namely periodicals, periodical indexing services, annuals or yearbooks, and annual review series.

Periodicals

Of the various types of serials, periodicals and their indexes occupy the top rank of importance in sci-tech libraries, primarily because of frequency (and hence currency) of publication and because information can be very specific. For example, it would be hard to find a book publisher willing to gamble on publishing a book on the narrow topic of aircraft brakes, but a periodical article on this subject would be welcomed by editors of appropriate periodicals, and they would not consider the topic too specific. As for being current, with periodicals issued frequently, some on a weekly basis, they can keep up to date with scholarly developments as well as news items about a discipline and its people.

There are many ways to classify periodicals, such as subject matter, country of origin, sponsorship, level of readership, and language. A few of these different criteria will be used here to give a broad outline of the many types of journals available.

Research-oriented Journals—Such periodicals are often sponsored by scientific or engineering societies, although many important titles are published by commercial firms and a few by government agencies. They are written primarily for experienced practitioners or scholars in the fields. Readers with less qualified backgrounds probably could not comprehend many of their articles. They rarely carry advertising, manuscripts submitted are usually referred by selected anonymous specialists before being accepted for publication, and there are usually many references to related publications cited. Some societies publish one general interest research journal plus a number of publications sponsored by subgroups of the parent organization. The Institute of Electrical and Electronics Engineers, for example, publishes not only a Proceedings, with technical articles covering all areas of membership interest, but also Transactions for over thirty special interest groups, ranging from technical writing to microwaves. Research-oriented journals can be found printed in any language; a few are multilingual, having abstracts in English and other languages.

Many of these journals are restricted to one major discipline, such as chemistry, geology, civil engineering, or mathematics, while others, just as highly regarded, might be limited to subtopics of the larger disciplines. Examples of the latter include organic chemistry, nuclear physics, seismology, or heat transfer. Then there are a handful of journals, exemplified in the English language by *Nature* and *Science,* which cover all disciplines of science and are often considered by scientists as the most desirable journals in which to have a brief communication published giving highlights of their recent research. It is the surest way in the scientific world to reach one's colleagues quickly, and being first in disclosing some major discovery in their columns is a feather in the scientist's cap. While many other fine journals cover all of science, none seems to rival these two in prominence. Engineering does not have any multifaceted journal with stature similar to these two, although multidisciplinary journals for engineering have existed for decades.

Trade Journals—Although an exact definition is not easy to prepare, in general a trade journal is one which deals on a less theoretical or broad-based level with a discipline and is restricted to emphasis on applications, usually in a narrow field. They deal more with engineering and applied science than with pure science. Examples include such topics as applied leather chemistry, metal working, the rubber trade, or plastic product manufacturing. Their articles appeal to a specialized audience, the journals invariably include advertising, and they have a shorter useful life in most collections. They serve a very practical purpose, entirely different, however, from titles devoted to basic research.

Brief Communication Journals—Because of the great urgency of scientists to get new discoveries placed in print as soon as possible, recent years have seen the emergence of a new breed of periodical. The contents of such a journal are entirely in the form of brief communications, describing what the writers believe to be first public announcements of new discoveries. Entries are limited in length, and only the highlights of the material can be given. Nevertheless, these journals receive great attention in their respective fields. They are limited in appeal to specialists in the subjects involved, particularly because they are necessarily too cryptic in style to inform a person not well versed in the subject.

Most of these journals are for the sciences and are limited to one discipline, such as physics or chemistry. The brief communications section of *Nature* and *Science* in a sense places them in this category, although these journals also contain a host of other features, such as feature articles.

General Purpose Journals—Periodicals that cover broad aspects of science and/or engineering, written for a wide audience, are to be found in many languages. However, only a few have what could be called a large audience. *Scientific American* is the best known journal which attempts to cover all types of science, and which is written for a wide range of readers, including the layman. Book reviews are one useful section in this publication. Once again, some aspects of *Nature* and *Science* qualify them for this category also. *Science,* for example, has a very good coverage of such topics as science and society, science and government, or science and youth.

News-Item Journals—In order to cover all the happenings involving scientists and engineers and the organizations for which they work, some special journals devote most of their space to information of this sort. They might list new appointments of persons, mergers, or formation of new research and engineering firms, awarding of contracts to agencies, recent statistics involving an industry, implications of new legislation on engineering projects, and a host of other topics. These journals may contain an occasional article, but generally the contributions are short and aim at timeliness rather than having in-depth research. Aside from portions of a journal like *Science* which contains such data, most of these periodicals (such as *Chemical and Engineering News, Engineering News Record,* and *Datamation*) are limited to a certain discipline. They meet a real need for those requiring or desiring this sort of information, even if the contents are largely ephemeral.

Other Types of Journals—Among the many ways to categorize journals, one is by language, which leads to a special type—cover-to-cover translations. These came to life in the last two decades, primarily because of the upsurge of interest in Soviet publications during their initial successes in astronautics. Because of the poor linguistic ability of many American scientists and engineers, particularly with regard to Russian, there was a rather sudden growth of such translated journals, followed by a few titles for Japanese material. If conditions permit, translated Chinese journals will probably appear fairly soon. Although the price of translated journals is high compared to original-language journals, the cost is low compared to what it would cost to have only a portion of one issue translated, especially by a skilled translator. Their contents range from those devoted to a large discipline, such as physics, to rather specific subjects, such as solar energy.

Keeping abreast of the many periodicals in print is no easy task, so one interesting type of journal is known as a current awareness periodical. It consists of reproductions of the contents pages of many periodicals, photo-reduced so that the format is compact and easy to handle. A firm responsible for publishing several of these journals issues them in particular categories, such as physical and chemical sciences, engineering, or the life sciences. They serve as an excellent way to scan the contents pages of hundreds of journals quickly, although the reader then, of course, has the task of obtaining a copy of the articles of interest. A tear sheet is also provided by the publisher (Institute for Scientific Information) to aid the reader not having local access to the periodicals.

Another type of journal which has limited uses but serves a purpose is the house organ—a publication of a commercial company or other organization. Some are prepared on a very high level, with carefully written material that is useful on a tutorial basis. Others are little more than glorified advertising brochures in periodical form. They are generally written for the specific trade or application of the sponsor. Most generate little interest in research circles.

Sci-tech libraries at universities may be expected to keep a few selected titles of another type of periodical—those prepared by universities and technical institutes to feature activities on their campuses. Some professors find them useful in keeping abreast of academic news from related schools, and students at times may find them interesting. They have a wide range of quality, however.

No doubt many other types could be identified, but the major ones have at least been described. The lists which follow give only a few titles to illustrate each type since there are thousands of periodicals that involve science/technology subjects.

This discussion on periodicals cannot terminate without describing some of the recent questioning of their role and their future. This is a subject which has attracted the attention of the publishers and sponsors of the journals and of their readers. Part of this analysis of the role of periodicals has come about because of financial problems. Rising costs, continued proliferation of new titles (some unnecessarily created, many scientists and engineers feel), and declining subscriptions have jointly caused many people to speculate as to whether periodicals can or should continue in their present format.

At one extreme are those who recommend discontinuation of journals as they now exist and their replacement with computer-controlled SDI services. Subscribers would receive only those papers that match their interest profile—much like the operation of computer-based data bank services providing current awareness service. At the other extreme are those who want no part of such a fragmentation and who want journals to continue as they are. The in-between group is considering alternatives to both extremes. An article discussing such alternatives mentions the use of reduced-size print for certain less essential portions of articles (e.g., preparation techniques for articles on chemistry) to save space, with even less essential material being published separately on microfiche, available to those interested upon applying for each item of interest.[1] Attempts to publish synopses of articles in lieu of complete versions met with very little acceptance by those involved in the experiment. Another worthwhile discussion of the future of scientific and technical journals touched on the subjects of cost reduction, alternative methods of publication, and social implications.[2]

A handful of journals are being published now only on microfiche, but they are either very specialized in scope or are confined to data supplementary to other publications.

Compounding the problem of financing periodicals is the question of photocopying. Many publishers are convinced that their budgetary problems cannot be solved until or unless they are reimbursed whenever their articles are photocopied, both by libraries and by individuals. The matter is very complex, and is now tied up in legal and governmental circles. Unquestionably, the existence of photocopies has reduced the number of subscribers to journals, particularly when one considers duplicate copies going to the same institution or group. The prices of subscriptions keep rising, which causes more libraries to reduce their subscription lists, thus creating a vicious circle that neither publishers, readers, nor librarians want to experience. At this stage the picture is very cloudy, and all parties involved are seeking a practical solution.

As for replacement of periodicals with separately selected and distributed papers, this would not be at all workable for certain periodicals, such as those devoted to news items or topics of general interest. No money could possibly be saved by mailing virtually every subscriber essentially the same material. The only application of this plan worth considering would be for scholarly journals with rather long articles on distinct topics, easily tied with interest profiles of particular readers. Even so, libraries would still need complete sets of the papers, since predicting the ones needed in the future would be literally impossible except in the case of very specialized collections, which are more apt to occur in special libraries than at universities.

Lists of Journals

Bibliographic Guide for Editors & Authors. Columbus, Ohio: Chemical Abstracts Service, 1974. 362 p.

> Published jointly with Engineering Index, Inc., and BioSciences Information Service of Biological Abstracts. Lists nearly twenty-eight thousand titles of scientific and technical journals, of which about two-thirds are still currently published. Indicates which are indexed by the three indexing services sponsoring the publication. Gives title abbreviations, CODEN, and International Standard Serial Numbers (ISSN) when available.

World List of Scientific Periodicals, Published in the Years 1900-1960. 4th ed. Edited by Peter Brown and G. B. Stratton. Washington, D.C.: Butterworths, 1963-1965. 3 vols.

> Covers nearly sixty thousand journals, giving title, commencement date, place of publication, and holdings of selected British libraries. Updated now by *British Union-Catalogue of Periodicals.*

Research Journals

Society-Sponsored

American Chemical Society
  Journal
  Also several specific titles, such as
    Analytical Chemistry
American Institute of Chemical Engineers
  Papers
American Institute of Industrial Engineers
  Transactions
American Institute of Physics
  Physical Review
American Mathematical Society
  Transactions
American Nuclear Society
  Transactions

American Psychological Association
  Psychological Bulletin
American Society of Civil Engineers
  Journals of various divisions:
      Construction
      Hydraulics
      Sanitary Engineering
      Power
      etc.
American Society of Mechanical Engineers
  Transactions (having specific titles):
      Journal of Applied Mechanics
      Journal of Engineering
      Journal of Heat Transfer
Botanical Society of America
  American Journal of Botany
Geological Society of America
  Bulletin
Institute of Electrical and Electronics Engineers
  Proceedings
  Transactions of various groups:
      Circuit Theory
      Geoscience Electronics
      Reliability
      Vehicular Technology
      etc.
Society of Mining Engineers
  Transactions
Society of Petroleum Engineers
  Journal

Commercial Sponsors

Deep-Sea Research (Pergamon)
International Journal of Heat and Mass Transfer
  (Pergamon)
Journal of Mathematical Psychology (Academic)
Journal of Molecular Biology (Academic)

Journal of Pure and Applied Algebra (North Holland)
Vacuum (Pergamon)

General Interest Journals

Bioscience (American Institute of Biological Scientists)
Geotimes (American Geological Institute)
Nature (Macmillan Journals, Ltd.)
New Scientist (B. Dixon)
Physics Today (American Institute of Physics)
Psychology Today (CRM, Inc.)
Science (American Association for the Advancement of Science)
Scientific American (Scientific American, Inc.)

News-Item Journals

Chemical & Engineering News (American Chemical Society)
Datamation (Technical Publishing)
Engineering News-Record (McGraw-Hill)

Current Awareness Journals (Contents pages)

Current contents (Institute for Scientific Information)
　Agriculture, Biology & Environmental Sciences
　Engineering & Technology
　Life Sciences
　Physical & Chemical Sciences

Brief Communication Journals

Applied Physics Letters (American Institute of Physics)
Information Processing Letters (North Holland)

Periodical Indexing and Abstracting Services

Without a periodical abstracting or indexing service, the use of periodicals would be tremendously handicapped. One would have to leaf through countless journals to find anything, and most users would soon give up in disgust. Fortunately, we are not faced with this problem. The sci-tech world is blessed with some of the finest tools of this sort of any discipline, much more numerous and specifically oriented than those in other fields, such as the humanities or the social services. These latter disciplines may in time catch up with the services in the sci-tech field, but this is unlikely.

Sci-tech indexing services are highly regarded because scientists and engineers need them so badly. Hence, financial support is forthcoming for well-designed services. Although *Chemical Abstracts* now costs over $2,000 per year, no librarian could conceive of trying to operate a chemistry library without a set. The same could be said of services in other fields—they are indispensable to the appropriate libraries. The costs may be high, but there is no practical substitute. The advent of computer-based data banks may eliminate some of the use of services for current awareness, but many queries can be answered just as quickly, if not more quickly, by use of indexes. Retrospective searches going back several years can, in many cases, be answered only by the use of printed indexes, since the computer files do not cover older years.

The quality of the services, like any other type of literature, varies widely. Some are prompt in their appearance, others are often late; some have abstracts and some do not; some are very readable and attractive and others are not. They have widely varied scopes, ranging from those covering all of science and engineering to those restricted to only one discipline (such as physics) or one portion of one discipline (such as highway engineering). Some cover all the periodicals they index from cover to cover, including news items, personnel and statistical items, and feature articles on any subject. Others give primary attention to certain key journals, but also include items selected from any journal they wish. Some have author indexes; some do not. Abstracts may vary from those which merely highlight the article (indicative abstracts) to annotations which give detailed information (informative abstracts).

Science and Engineering (General)

Applied Science and Technology Index. New York: H. W. Wilson, 1958-   . Monthly.

Covers all aspects of engineering and applied science. There are no annotations. No author index. Often uses several subject headings for each article. Over two hundred periodicals are indexed, usually including all articles and features, such as biographical sketches, price data, and statistics. There are quarterly and annual cumulations. Confined to English language journals, mostly U.S. A very useful service in spite of its lack of abstracts and author index. Is relatively inexpensive and is found in many libraries, including some where science is not a major interest.

Science Citation Index. Philadelphia, Pa.: Institute for Scientific Information, 1961-   . Quarterly.

Provides an index to the references cited in current periodical articles in over twenty-four hundred scientific and technical periodicals. It allows one to determine the reference use made of an older article in more recent years, among other features. Has annual cumulations. A five-year cumulation exists for 1965-1969. All versions have separate personal author and corporate author indexes. A companion publication, *Permuterm Index,* allows a conventional subject approach. Also available on magnetic tape.

Aeronautics and Astronautics

International Aerospace Abstracts. New York: American Institute of Aeronautics and Astronautics, Inc., 1961-   . Monthly.

Sponsored by NASA. Covers aeronautics and space science. Indexes periodicals, books, and conference papers, using indicative abstracts. Each issue has author, subject, contract number, and report number indexes, which cumulate semiannually and annually. Scans over twelve hundred journals for items to index. Serves as a companion volume to *Scientific and Technical Aerospace Reports* (which see).

Biology

Biological Abstracts. Philadelphia, Pa.: BioSciences Information Service of Biological Abstracts, 1927-   . Semimonthly.

Covers a wide range of subjects, including botany, zoology,

the aerial parts of each plant are determined, "leaf are product"/plant may be calculated by recording the product of the length and maximum width of each leaf and obtaining the total value/plant. By comparing results for plants of the same porgeny grown in contaminated and un-

contaminated compost it is possible to recognize progenies which are significantly smaller as a result of infection. Plants which are not reduced in size in contaminated compost are usually infected but appear to be tolerant of the presence of the pathogen.--E. M. D.

PLANT PHYSIOLOGY, BIOCHEMISTRY and BIOPHYSICS

See also: Aero-Space and Underwater Biological Effects
 Agronomy
 Biochemistry
 Biophysics
 Chemotherapy - Antifungal Agents
 Circadian Rhythm and Other Periodic Cycles
 Cytology and Cytochemistry - Plant
 Ecology (Environmental Biology) - Plant
 Forestry and Forest Products
 Genetics and Cytogenetics - Plant
 Horticulture
 Immunology (Immunochemistry) - Bacterial, Viral and Fungal
 Medical and Clinical Microbiology (includes Veterinary) -
  Mycology, Phycology
 Microorganisms, General (includes Protista)
 Pest Control, General (includes Plants and Animals); Pesti-
  cides; Herbicides
 Phytopathology
 Soil Microbiology

APPARATUS AND METHODS

See also: Methods, Materials and Apparatus, General
 Microbiological Apparatus, Methods and Media

33811. MIFLIN, BENJAMIN J.* and HARRY BEEVERS. (Dep. Biochem., Rothamstead Exp. Stn., Harpenden, Herts AL5 2JQ, Engl., UK.)
Isolation of intact plastids from a range of plant tissues. PLANT
PHYSIOL 53(6): 870-874. Illus. 1974. [In Engl. with Engl. summ.]
--A technique for the isolation of intact plastids from spinach (Spinacia
oleracea) and pea (Pisum sativum) leaves, pea roots and castor bean
(Ricinus communis) endosperm is described. This technique involves
brief centrifugation of whole homogenates on density gradients. Intact
plastids were located in the gradient by assaying for triose phosphate
isomerase activity. Contamination of the plastid peak with mitochondria and microbodies was estimated by measurement of cytochrome
oxidase and catalase, respectively. For 3 of the 4 tissues the level of
contamination of the plastids by these organelles was 2% or less. The
sedimentation behavior of microbodies from different tissues is discussed.

33812. SCHOLL, R. L.*, J. E. HARPER and R. H. HAGEMAN. (Dep.
Genet., Ohio State Univ., Columbus, Ohio 43210, USA.) Improvements
of the nitrite color development in assays of nitrate reductase by
phenazine methosulfate and zinc acetate. PLANT PHYSIOL 53(6):
825-828. Illus. 1974. [In Engl. with Engl. summ.]--Nitrate reductase
activity is most commonly assayed by measurement of product formation. Excess NADH and factor(s) presented in the enzyme extract
that interfere with the diazotization and zinc color complex of NO_2
caused a depression of apparent nitrate reductase activity. Two post-
assay treatments were found that markedly enhanced the extent of NO_2
color formation and apparent nitrate reductase activity [in Zea mays
and Glycine max]. The procedure involves stopping the reaction with
zinc acetate (50 µmol/ml of reaction mix), followed by removal of
the precipitate by centrifugation. Presumably the zinc acetate removes
extract factor(s) that interfere with color development, because it does
not remove the NADH. Phenazine methosulfate (15 nmoles/ml of reaction mix) is added to aliquots of the supernatant and allowed to stand
for 20 min at 30°C to oxidize the residual NADH before color development.

33813. GREEN, ANITA A. and PETER C. NEWELL. (Dep. Biochem.,
Univ. Oxf., Oxford CX1 3QU, Engl., UK.) The isolation and sub-
fractionation of plasma membrane from the cellular slime mold
Dictyostelium discoideum. BIOCHEM J 140(2): 313-322. Illus.
1974. [In Engl. with Engl. summ.]--A procedure for the isolation and
separation of 3 different subfractions of plasma membrane from the
cellular slime mold D. discoideum is described. The cells were
disrupted by freeze-thawing in liquid N_2 and plasma membranes were
purified by equilibrium centrifugation in a sucrose gradient. The cell
surface was labeled with radioactive iodide by using the lactoperoxidase
iodination method. Alkaline phosphatase was identified as a plasma-
membrane marker by its co-distribution with [125I]iodide. 5'-Nucleo-
tidase, which has been widely described as a plasma-membrane marker
enzyme in mammalian tissues, was not localized to any marked extent
in D. discoideum plasma membrane. The isolated plasma membranes

showed a 24-fold enrichment of alkaline phosphatase specific activity
relative to the homogenate and a yield of 50% of the total plasma
membranes. Determination of succinate dehydrogenase and NADPH-
cytochrome c reductase activities indicated that the preparation contained 2% of the total mitochondria and 3% of the endoplasmic reticul-
um. When the plasma-membrane preparation was further disrupted
in a tight-fitting homogenizer, 3 plasma-membrane subfractions of
different densities were obtained by isopycnic centrifugation. The
enrichment of alkaline phosphatase was greatest in the subfraction with
the lowest density. This fraction was enriched 36-fold relative to the
homogenate and contained 19% of the total alkaline phosphatase activity
but only 0.08% of the succinate dehydrogenase activity and 0.34% of
the NADPH-cytochrome c reductase activity. Electron microscopy
of this fraction showed it to consist of smooth membrane vesicles with
no recognizable contaminants.

33814. KOKYRTSA, P. N. (Bot. Gard., Acad. Sci. Mold. SSR,
Kishinev, USSR.) O kul'tivirovanii sinezelenykh vodoroslei. [Cultiva-
tion of blue- green algae.] GIDROBIOL ZH 9(4): 75-78. 1973. [In
Russ.]--The purpose of the investigation was to cultivate species of
blue-green algae most characteristic for bodies of waters on Moldavia
[USSR], and to select optimal media for their development. Natural
populations of Microcystis aeruginosa f. aeruginosa, Pseudanabaena
galeata f. galeata, Oscillatoria agardhii f. agardhii and Oscillatoria
brevis f. brevis were studied. To obtain a sufficient biomass of pure
cultures in a reasonably short time (10—14 days) it is expedient to
use Chu medium No. 10 as modified by Gerloff. In long (more than 20
days) physiological and biochemical investigations, Fitzgerald medium
No. 11 as modified by Zehender and Gorham should be used.--M. D. S.

33815. LUPATOV, V. M., I. A. TRIFONOVA, E. A. AFANAS'EV
and V. M. KUTYURIN. (V. I. Vernadskii Inst. Geochem. Anal. Chem.,
Acad. Sci. USSR, Moscow, USSR.) Metod skorostnoi differentsial'noi
kulonometrii v issledovaniyakh kinetiki vydeleniya kisloroda pri
impul'snom osveshchenii rastenii. [The technique of high-speed
differential coulombmetry applied for the investigation of kinetics of
oxygen evolution during impulsive illumination of the plants.]
FIZIOL RAST 20(6): 1295-1299. Illus. 1973[recd. 1974]. [In Russ.
with Russ. and Engl. summ.]--A method was presented for the registration of O_2 of photosynthesis in the course of the impulsive illumination
of the cells. The theoretical basis of the technique and the functional
diagram of the equipment were described. The evidence suggest 3
reactions necessary for the evolution of O_2 by the cells and chloroplasts.
The technique could be applied for the investigation of the kinetics of
the evolution of O_2 of photosynthesis during the impulsive illumination
of the plants.

33816. BRUNI, ALESSANDRO and GIAN LUIGI VANNINI. (Ist. Bot.,
Univ. Ferrara, Ferrara, Italy.) Possibilità d'impeigo dell'acridina
e dell'acriflavina nella ricera istochimica dei polisaccaridi insolubili
della cellula vegetale. [Possible use of acridine orange and acriflavine
in histochemistry studies of plant cell insoluble polysaccharides.]
G BOT ITAL 107(4): 201-206. 1973[recd. 1974]. [In Ital. with Ital.
and Engl. summ.]--The 2 dyes can give, under certain conditions,
specific metachromatic effects. A discussion of the results and a
comparison with those obtained by PAS (periodic acid Schiff) are
included.--J. S. J.

33817. JANOVICOVA, JINDRA*, STEFAN BLECHA* and JAN
SUPUKA. (Vysk. Ustav Hyg., ul Cs, Armady 40, Bratislava, Czech.)
Meranie plochy listov fotoplanimetrom. [Measuring of leaf area by
means of a photoplanimeter.] BIOLOGIA (BRATISL) 29(1): 61-67.
Illus. 1974. [In Czech with Czech, Engl. and Russ. summ.]--Leaf
area can be estimated in the region of regressive straight line (up to
57.68 cm^2) with the accuracy of + 0.11 cm^2, and in the region of regressive curve (over 67.68 cm^2) with the accuracy of + 0.52 cm^2. Large
leaves can be divided up into smaller parts and their area can be expressed as the sum of the measured partial areas. The productive
yield in case of leaves that need not be divided up is as much as 150
leaves/h. The device can be used for measuring leaf areas of woody
plants, herbs, grasses, germination leaves, etc.--H. R.

CHEMICAL CONSTITUENTS

See also: Pharmacognosy and Pharmaceutical Botany
 Plant Physiology, Biochemistry and Biophysics - Apparatus
  and Methods, Enzymes, Growth Substances, Metabolism

Figure 3   *Biological Abstracts* sample page. (Reproduced with the permission of the copyright owner, Biological Abstracts, Inc. © 1974.)

biochemistry, physiology, soils, and psychiatry. Has detailed abstracts. Each issue has an author index, a KWIC-type of subject index, and various other special ones. (For a sample of this service, see figure 3.) Also available on microfilm and magnetic tape. Indexes cumulate semiannually. A companion volume is *Bioresearch Index*, issued since 1968 as an index to symposia, reports, trade journals, etc.

Chemistry and Chemical Engineering

Chemical Abstracts. Columbus, Ohio: American Chemical Society, 1907- . Weekly.

An excellent abstracting service which indexes over twelve thousand journals, patents from more than twenty countries, new books, reports, and conference proceedings. Has excellent informative abstracts giving considerable detail, such as names of all compounds, quantities, instruments used. Has weekly and semiannual author, subject, and patent indexes. Also available are quinquennial (five-year) and decennial indexes (for the period 1907-1956). Other indexes include those for formulas, an index to ring systems, and a registry (chemical) number index. Available in microfilm as well as magnetic tape (in modified form). Annually indexes around half a million items, grouped into eighty subject categories. Covers a wide range of subjects in addition to pure chemistry, e.g., metallurgy, chemical engineering, solid state studies. Can be obtained in one or more of five sections for those not wishing the entire set. (For a sample page of this service, see figure 4.)

Computers and Data Processing

Computer and Control Abstracts. London: Institution of Electrical Engineers, 1966- . Monthly.

A joint publication of the Institute of Electrical and Electronics Engineers and its British counterpart. Issued as Part C of *Science Abstracts*. Items have indicative abstracts, and are arranged by a classification plan. Each issue has separate author, patent, con-

administered s.c. at 125 mg/kg or i.p. at 65 mg/kg completely eliminated *T. crassicauda* parasites from host rats, and had no apparent hematol. or morphol. effects on the rats. *Tetramisole* **[6649-23-6]** and *SKF 29044* **[14255-87-9]** were partially active against the parasite, whereas piperazine, dichlorvos, disophenol, niridazole, thiabendazole, and pyrantel were without significant activity. Twenty male-female breeding pairs and 22 harem mated groups were infected with *T. crassicauda*. Forty-one of the 42 groups and their 1st 3 consecutive litters were cleared of the parasite by I treatment. Comparison of indices such as mean birth wt., mean weaning wt., and mean no. of neonates per litter gave no evidence of I teratol. toxicity.

142853k Effects of carbachol on water and electrolyte fluxes and transepithelial electrical potential differences of the rabbit submaxillary main duct perfused in vitro. Martin, C. J.; Froemter, E.; Gebler, B.; Knauf, H.; Young, J. A. (Max-Planck-Inst. Biophys., Frankfurt/M., Ger.). *Pfluegers Arch.* **1973**, *341*(2), 131-42 (Eng). *Carbachol* **[51-83-2]** partially depolarized the transepithelial potential difference and decreased net water, *Na* **[7440-23-5]**, and *chloride* **[16887-00-6]** reabsorption in the rabbit submaxillary main duct perfused in vivo and in vitro with HCO₃⁻ saline. Transport of *K* **[7440-09-7]** and *bicarbonate* **[71-52-3]** in the duct was not affected. In vitro carbachol was effective in concns. as low as $10^{-7}M$ and perhaps lower. *Atropine* **[51-55-8]** completely blocked the effects of carbachol present at twice the atropine concn. Carbachol apparently decreases the Na conductance of the luminal face of the duct epithelial cell. This response was secondary to an undefined primary action of carbachol on the interstitial face of the cell.

142854m Inhibition of p-chlorophenoxyisobutyrate by 1-methyl-2-mercaptoimidazole and related compounds. Ryan, Norman T.; Richert, Dan A.; Westerfeld, Wilfred W. (Upstate Med. Cent., State Univ. New York, Syracuse, N. Y.). *Biochem. Pharmacol.* **1973**, *22*(12), 1397-404 (Eng). The

hypolipidemic drug *p-chlorophenoxyisobutyrate* **(I)** **[882-09-7]** enhanced the induction of both rat liver mitochondrial *α-glycerophosphate dehydrogenase* **[9001-49-4]** and sol. *malic enzyme* **[9028-47-1]** by thyroid hormone. The intensification of the thyroxin (T₄) **[51-48-9]** induction by I was blocked by simultaneous administration of the goitrogen, *1-methyl-2-mer= captoimidazole* **[60-56-0]**, and related compds. such as *1-methylimidazole* **[616-47-7]**, *imidazole* **[288-32-4]** and *thiourea* **[62-56-6]**. However, the effect of I in preventing an *orotic acid* **[65-86-1]**-induced fatty liver or intensifying the β-lipoprotein band in serum gel electrophoresis was not inhibited by imidazole. I may also affect lipid metab. by a mechanism unrelated to the thyroid hormone.

142855n Rat uterine contractility and the activities of uterine adenyl cyclase and phosphodiesterase during the estrus cycle. Sim, Meng Kwoon; Chantharaksri, Udom (Dep. Pharmacol., Mahidol Univ., Bangkok, Thailand). *Biochem. Pharmacol.* **1973**, *22*(12), 1417-22 (Eng). *Theophylline* **(I)**

[58-55-9] at 50 mg/100 ml inhibited rat uterine contractions produced in response to *oxytocin* **[50-56-6]**. I inhibition of oxytocin-induced max. uterine contractions was greatest at early metestrus. The oxytocin concn. producing 40% max. contraction in the presence and absence of I ((oxytoxin (E₄₀) + I)/oxytoxin (E₄₀)) was also the highest at early metestrus. The activities of *adenyl cyclase* **[9012-42-4]** and *phosphodiesterase* **[9025-82-5]** increased from 2.52 p-moles/min/mg protein and 1.90 nmoles/= min/mg protein, resp., at proestrus to 15 p-moles/min/mg protein and 5 nmoles/min/mg protein at metestrus, and then fell until the following proestrus. At early metestrus, cellular turnover of *cyclic AMP* **[60-92-4]** may be high and the exaggerated inhibition of oxytocyin-induced max. contraction may be due to extensive accumulation of cyclic AMP produced from I inhibition of phosphodiesterase.

142856p Effect of 4-phenyl-3-isocoumarincarboxylic acid and some of its derivatives on blood clotting. Arrigo Reina, R.; Scoto, G. M. (Ist. Farmacol., Univ. Catania, Catania, Italy). *Farmaco, Ed. Sci.* **1973**, *28*(6), 478-84 (Ital). A series of coumarin derivs., including *Na 4-phenyl-3-isocoumarincarbox= ylate* **(I)** **[42062-05-5]**, *N-allyl-4-phenyl-3-isocoumarincarb= oxamide* **[41571-18-0]**, *N-isopropyl-4-phenyl-3-isocoumarinca=

rboxamide **[41056-63-7]**, *2-dimethylaminoethyl 4-phenyl-3-is= ocoumarincarboxylate* **[42062-08-8]**, and *2-diethylaminoethyl-4-= phenyl-3-isocoumarincarboxylate* **[42062-09-9]**, injected i.p. into rats at doses as low as 0.2 mg/kg, decreased the Quick time, the Howell time, and the blood recalcification time. Although these compds. were able to increase the coagulability of the blood even at low doses in vivo, no alteration of coagulation was seen in vitro.

142857q Mechanism of action of cerebroventricularly perfused phentolamine on carotid occlusion response in cats. Abraham, G. J. S.; Tikare, S. S.; Ahmed, S. S. (Dep. Pharmacol., Goa Med. Coll., Panaji, India). *Indian J. Med. Res.* **1973**, *61*(6), 896-902 (Eng). Studies on stereotaxic

stimulation of the medulla and hypothalamus and cannulation of the vertebral artery and aqueduct in anesthetized cats showed the medulla to be the site of action of cerebroventricularly perfused *phentolamine* **(I)** **[50-60-2]** (50–100 ng/kg/min). Preinjection (cerebroventricular) of *hemicholinium* **[16478-59-4]** (1 mg/kg) or *atropine* **[51-55-8]** (5 μg/kg) did not affect I depressant action, thereby eliminating the possibility of acetylcholine acting as neurotransmitter in I action in the carotid occlusion response. Depletion of brain catechol amine and serotonin levels prevented I action. I action was restored by *L-dopa* **[59-92-7]** but not by serotonin, thus indicating the adrenergic nature of I action.

142858r Effect of the association trimethoprim-sulfameth= oxazole in the experimental infection of mice by Toxoplasma gondii. Histological and immunohistological studies. Terragna, A.; Cellesi, C.; Barberi, A. (Ist. Clin. Mal. Infett., Univ. Siena, Siena, Italy). *Boll. Ist. Sieroter. Milan.* **1973**, *52*(1), 60-9 (Ital). *Trimethoprim-sulfamethoxazole mixt.* **(I–II**

mixt.) **[8064-90-2]** protected mice against infection by *T. gondii*. Examn. of the liver showed no histol. damage and no immunol. evidence of protozoa in the treated mice. I–II mixt. (2:10 mg or 4:20 mg/day) was given i.p. in divided doses each day for 20 days, beginning at the time of infection.

142859s Effect of the association trimethoprim-sulfameth= oxazole in the experimental infection of mice by Toxoplasma gondii. Histochemical study. Cellesi, C.; Barberi, A.; Terragna, A. (Ist. Clin. Mal. Infett., Univ. Siena, Siena, Italy). *Boll. Ist. Sieroter. Milan.* **1973**, *52*(1), 70-6 (Ital).

Trimethoprim-sulfamethoxazole mixt. (I–II mixt.) **[8064-90-2]** was effective in preventing infection by *T. gondii* in mice, although histochem. study of liver showed that some toxic damage resulted from the drug mixt. I–II mixt. (2:10 mg or 4:20 mg per day) was given i.p. in divided doses for 20 days, beginning at the time of infection.

142860k Interference of 3,4,5-trimethoxybenzoyl-γ-amino= butyric acid with the GABA-oxoglutarate reaction. Ariano, M. (Cent. Ric., Ist. Chemioter. Ital., San Grato di Lodi, Italy). *Riv. Farmacol. Ter.* **1973**, *4*(1), 133-40 (Ital). *3,4,5-Trimeth=*

ference paper, and book indexes, which cumulate annually. A three-year cumulative author and subject index is available.

Earth Sciences

Bibliography and Index of Geology. Boulder, Colo.: Geological Society of America, 1933- . Monthly.

Covers the subject on a global basis plus North American theses. In 1969 it became the successor to *Bibliography and Index of Geology Exclusive of North America.* Has annual author and subject indexes.

Bibliography of North American Geology. Washington, D.C.: U.S. Geological Survey, 1896- . Annual.

Issued as a USGS Bulletin. Arranged by author with a subject index. Covers the period 1732 to date.

Electrical Engineering

Electrical & Electronics Abstracts. London: Institution of Electrical Engineers, 1898- . Monthly.

Jointly published by the British society named above and the Institute of Electrical and Electronics Engineers. Issued as Part B of *Science Abstracts.* Has nearly informative abstracts. Each issue contains indexes for authors, bibliographies, books, conference proceedings, patents, and reports. Semiannual cumulative indexes are also issued. Over two thousand journals are partially indexed, while another hundred are indexed completely. Closely related to *Physics Abstracts* (Series A of *Science Abstracts*) (which see) and *Computer and Control Abstracts* (Series C of *Science Abstracts*) (which see).

Engineering (General)

Engineering Index. New York: Engineering Index, Inc., 1884- . Monthly.

Probably the most outstanding index to general engineering literature. Covers all aspects of the subject, has indicative abstracts, and includes a wide journal coverage (over twenty-two hundred publications). Indexes periodicals, society publications, and certain reports. Has an annual hardbound cumulation. All issues include an author index. Has many cross references. Also available in card form, on microfilm, and on magnetic tape (*Compendex*). (For a sample page of this service, see figure 5.)

Mathematics

Mathematical Reviews. Providence, R.I.: American Mathematical Society, 1940-   . Monthly.

Provides an annotated index to journals, plus a certain number of books, theses, etc. Each issue has an author index, which cumulates semiannually. Cumulative author indexes covering several years also exist.

Mechanical Engineering

Applied Mechanics Reviews. New York: American Society of Mechanical Engineers, 1947-   . Monthly.

Covers such topics as mechanics of solids, mechanics of fluids, automatic control, heat, rational mechanics, and mathematical methods. Has indicative abstracts, with author indexes in each issue. Cumulative author and keyword subject indexes are published annually.

Metals and Metal Working

Metals Abstracts. London: Institute of Metals, 1968-   . Monthly.

Published jointly by the Institute of Metals and the American Society for Metals, replacing their former publications, *Metallurgical Abstracts* and *Review of Metal Literature,* respectively. Has indicative abstracts. Each issue has an author

OSCILLATORS—Contd.

042973 ANALIZ USLOVII SAMOVOZBUZH-DENIYA AVTOGENERATOROV NA TUN-NEL'NYKH DIODAKH SO STABILIZATSIEI CHASTOTY. [Analysis of Self-Exciting Conditions of a Master Oscillator Using Tunnel Diodes with Stabilized Frequency]. 5 refs. In Russian.

Karlinskaya, B.N.; Karlinskii, S.I.; Tan'ko, A.V. *Izv Vyssh Uchebn Zaved Radioelektron* v 17 n 1 1974 p 74-79.

042974 RAPID SYNCHRONIZATION CIRCUIT FOR A PHASE-LOCK OSCILLATOR. A phase-lock oscillator is shown that senses when data of the correct frequency is present on a data input line, by counting the output of a voltage-controlled oscillator by frequency sense and counter logic. It also prevents locking on a harmonic of the input data by maintaining the frequency of the oscillator 14 at its nominal value, until data of the correct frequency exists at the data input, and also requires less synchronization time.

Shidler, K.A. *IBM Tech Disclosure Bull* v 16 n 11 Apr 1974 p 3719-3722.

042975 DIGITAL OSCILLATORS. Three TTL compatible oscillators are described, together with their frequency performance limits. One is suitable for clock-pulse generation, and the other two are low and high stability variable-frequency sources. Various refs.

Bell, J.F.W. Univ of Aston, Birmingham, Engl; Sharp, J.C.K.; Wong, Y. *Int J Electron* v 36 n 4 Apr 1974 p 565-570.

OSCILLATORS, GUNN

042976 ANALYTIC MODEL FOR VARACTOR-TUNED WAVEGUIDE GUNN OSCILLATORS. An analytic model for electronic tuning of a X-band waveguide transferred-electron oscillator is presented. The oscillator is electronically tunable by a varactor, and mechanically tunable by movement of a short circuit. The model is used to predict oscillation frequency, maximum electronic tuning range, and electronic tuning versus varactor bias voltage. Two different methods, the "zero reactance theory" and the Slater perturbation theory, are used to calculate the electronic tuning. The results of these calculations are compared to experimental results for two different oscillator configurations.

Templin, A.S. Purdue Univ, West Lafayette, Indiana; Gunshor, R.L. *IEEE Trans Microwave Theory Tech* v MTT-22 n 5 May 1974 p 554-556.

042977 UNDERSTANDING THE BASICS OF GUNN OSCILLATOR OPERATION. The electrons in GaAs can be in one of two conduction bands. One band happens to have a much higher mobility than the other. Electrons are initially in the high mobility band, but as the electric field is increased, more and more are scattered to the low mobility band. This mixture of electrons has an average velocity somewhere between the individual band velocities. As more electrons are scattered to the low mobility band, average velocity drops. The electric field where velocity begins to drop is called the threshold field. Both theory and experiment indicate that the threshold field in GaAs is 3.2 kv/cm. Since current is proportional to electron velocity and voltage is proportional to electric field, this means a GaAs resistor will have a region of negative resistance. A Gunn diode is then a GaAs resistor biased into the region of negative resistance. The layer thickness must be close to a "transit-time length" at the frequency of operation. This requirement is necessary in order to cause the proper phase relationship for negative resistance to occur between the voltage and current. A Gunn oscillator is made by mating a diode with a microwave circuit which provides positive resistance equal to the diode's negative resistance. Frequency of operation is determined by the resonance of this circuit.

Sweet, Allen A. Microwave Assoc Inc. *EDN* v 19 n 9 May 5 1974 p 40-47.

042978 METHOD OF IMPROVING TUNING RANGE OBTAINED FROM A VARACTOR-TUNED GUNN OSCILLATOR. It is proposed that the technique of reactance compensation, previously applied successfully to improve the bandwidth of parametric amplifiers, can be applied to varactor-tuned oscillators, such as Gunn oscillators, with significant improvement in the electronic-tuning range. 3 refs.

Aitchison, C.S. Chelsea Coll, London, Engl. *Electron Lett* v 10 n 7 Apr 4 1974 p 94-95.

OSCILLATORS, MICROWAVE See Also TELEVISION RECEIVERS.

042979 SINGLE-TUNED SOLID-STATE MICROWAVE OSCILLATORS. The incorporation of a lossy stabilizing element into a microwave oscillator circuit is described. Such an element facilitates the application of dc bias to the circuit, and makes it unlikely that oscillations occur at undesired frequencies. Configurations that have been used for solid-state oscillators at frequencies from 8 GHz to over 110 GHz are discussed. 8 refs.

Kenyon, N.D. Post Off Res Dep, Ipswich, Engl. *Int J Circuit Theory Appl* v 1 n 4 Dec 1973 p 387-393.

042980 MISE EN OEUVRE DES DIODES A AVALANCHE POUR HYPERFREQUENCES. [Use of Avalanche Diodes for Microwaves]. Operating an avalanche diode raises a problem of circuit design: the existing couplings between the microwave and low-frequency properties of the diode are recalled and the conditions that the bias circuit must meet—internal impedance and stabilization range—are examined as a function of the mode of operation. These considerations have been applied to a 5 W - 12 GHz multidiode source which has an 8% overall efficiency, including the bias circuit. This source is described, with its noise performance. 21 refs. In French.

Semichon, Alain Lab d'Electron et de Phys Appl, Limeil-Brevannes, Fr. *Acta Electron* v 17 n 2 Apr 1974 p 171-180.

042981 CIRCUIT ANALYSIS OF A STABLE AND LOW NOISE IMPATT-DIODE OSCILLATOR FOR X-BAND. This paper describes an Impatt-diode oscillator using a circuit first described by Kurokawa and Magalhaes. On the basis of a practical equivalent circuit representation conditions for maximum power and low noise will be derived. Using a Si N$^+$PP$^+$ diode an RMS frequency deviation of 0.8 Hz (in a 100 Hz band at 200 kHz from carrier) at 10 GHz has been obtained. The frequency-temperature behavior of the oscillator is found to be 10^{-6}°C^{-1}.

Tjassens, Hindrik Philips Res Lab, Eindhoven, Neth. *Acta Electron* v 17 n 2 Apr 1974 p 181-185.

042982 CHARACTERISTICS OF IMPATT DIODES IN RELATION TO WIDEBAND VARACTOR TUNED OSCILLATORS. Wideband varactor tuned oscillators require the varactor junction capacitance to provide the dominant reactance in the oscillator circuit. In addition, stray package and circuit reactances affect the tuning range which is eventually limited by the increased varactor power loss. These effects are particularly noticeable for the Impatt diode because the device has an inherently large Q factor. To understand these limitations, an accurately characterized wideband coaxial varactor tuned oscillator is presented.

Corbey, Colin D. Mullard Res Lab, Redhill, Surrey, Engl. *Acta Electron* v 17 n 2 Apr 1974 p 187-192.

Noise

042983 AM AND FM NOISE OF BARITT OSCILLATORS. Baseband, am, and fm noise of a BARITT diode oscillator in the range 100 Hz-50 kHz off the carrier has been measured under various operating conditions. A simple calculation has been made, relating the baseband noise to the oscillator am and fm noise via measured amplitude and frequency modulation sensitivities and the results have been compared with the noise measured. It should be noted that, depending on the bias current applied, both am and fm noise performance can be degraded by up-conversion. Complete removal of up-converted noise requires a high-impedance low-noise bias supply since both the diode noise a bias supply noise at baseband frequencies may be significant when up-converted. Even with all modulation suppressed, the am and fm noise has a flicker component almost completely correlated with the diode flicker noise at baseband frequencies. The rf power dependence of the am and fm noise has also been investigated. It is shown that the BARITT oscillator noise compared very favorably with that of IMPATT's and TEO's.

Fikart, Josef L. GTE Lenkurt, Burnaby, BC. *IEEE Trans Microwave Theory Tech* v MTT-22 n 5 May 1974 p 517-523.

Noise, Spurious Signal

042984 NOISE IN IMPATT-DIODE OSCILLATORS. The noise properties of low-Q Impatt-diode oscillators are discussed on the basis of two theories. The linear noise theory is based on linear amplification of avalanche current noise. It can be applied at low signal levels only. At high signal level a non-linear theory is needed. This theory is described with matrix algebra, the noise being considered as a perturbation of the noise-free situation. Within the respective ranges of signal levels where the theories may be expected to be applicable, the agreement with the experiments is satisfying. 30 refs.

Goedbloed, Jasper J. Philips Res Lab, Eindhoven, Neth; Vlaardingerbroek, Marinus T. *Acta Electron* v 17 n 2 Apr 1974 p 151-163.

OSCILLATORS, PARAMETRIC

042985 CHARACTERISTICS OF THE OPTICAL PARAMETRIC OSCILLATOR AND ITS USE FOR SELECTIVE EXCITATION. Techniques are presented for obtaining stable, single mode output from an optical parametric oscillator and for aligning such an oscillator with a molecular or atomic transition. A line width of 10^{-3} cm^{-1} or less was obtained with a long term frequency stability of 10^{-3} cm^{-1} or better. It has been demonstrated that an OPO can stay aligned for several hours with an absorption line of half-width 0.01 cm^{-1}. 6 refs.

Hordvik, Audun Air Force Cambridge Res Lab, Bedford, Mass; Sackett, Philip B. *Appl Opt* v 13 n 4 May 1974 p 1060-1064.

OSCILLOSCOPES, CATHODE RAY See Also COMPUTER PERIPHERAL EQUIPMENT.

042986 SIMPLE TECHNIQUE FOR DISPLAYING PERIODICALLY JITTERED BINARY WAVEFORMS. A display system is described that electrically transforms a periodically jittered binary waveform to enable the modulating signal to be viewed directly on an oscilloscope, without demodulation.

Del Monte, H.W. Post Off Res Dep, London, Engl. *Electron Lett* v 10 n 5 Mar 7 1974 p 52-53.

OVENS, INDUSTRIAL See Also PROTECTIVE COATINGS—Vacuum Application.

Control See OSCILLATORS.

Exhaust Gases

042987 UNTERSUCHUNGEN DES REINIGUNGSEFFEKTES GASBETRIEBENER THERMISCHER NACHVERBRENNUNGEN AN ABGASEN VON KAFFEEROESTEREIEN. [Investigating the Cleaning Effect of Gas-Fired Post-Combustion Chambers on Waste Gas From Coffee Bean Roasting]. Investigation results of exhaust gases from a coffee roasting oven are presented. It was found that odor is dependent upon the contents of hydrocarbons, aldehydes and organic acids. The use of a post-combustion chamber operating at about 650 deg. C makes it possible to reduce the percentage of the above mentioned constituents to an extent where the waste gas is free from odor. Using a newly designed post-combustion chamber, a concentration far below the above upper limit was

index. A companion volume to *Metals Abstracts Index*, a monthly publication containing a subject index (plus the same author index). Cumulative author and subject indexes are issued. Covers over twelve hundred journals, with around twenty-five thousand items indexed annually. Also available on magnetic tapes.

Mining and Minerals

IMM Abstracts. London: Institution of Mining and Metallurgy, 1950-   . Bimonthly.

Deals with mining, mineral dressing, and economic geology. Arranged by a subject classification system. All items are annotated, with abstracts tending to be more informative than indicative.

Ocean Engineering and Oceanography

Oceanic Abstracts. La Jolla, Calif.: Pollution Abstracts, Inc., 1964-   . Bimonthly.

Covers all aspects of oceans, including topics concerning biology, geology, meteorology, fishing, pollution, etc. Some items have brief abstracts and include a list of keywords for each item indexed. An author index and a keyword index appear in each issue and cumulate annually.

Physics

Physics Abstracts. London: Institution of Electrical Engineers, 1898-   . Semimonthly.

Covers all aspects of physics thoroughly and is Part A of *Science Abstracts*. All items are annotated. Each issue has a separate author index. Semiannual indexes for authors and subjects exist, as well as five-year cumulative indexes for authors and subjects. Current awareness service and magnetic tapes are also available.

Pollution

Pollution Abstracts. La Jolla, Calif.: Pollution Abstracts, Inc., 1970-   .
Bimonthly.

Includes all types of pollution—air, water, solid waste, and
noise, as well as radiation, pesticides, and general environmental
quality. Each issue has an author and KWIC subject index, which
cumulate annually. Covers journals plus selected conference
proceedings, papers, and reports.

Psychology

Psychological Abstracts. Washington, D.C.: American Psychological
Association, 1927-   . Monthly.

Includes selected monographs and reports in addition to serial
literature. Has author and subject indexes, some of which are
cumulated for several years. Data since 1967 also available on
magnetic tape.

Annuals and Yearbooks

Yearbooks, like annuals, are usually issued on an annual basis; both
are largely statistical, although not exclusively. Some have regular
reviews in prose form along with statistical data. On the other hand,
annual supplements to encyclopedias are almost entirely in prose form,
with statistics playing little or no part in their contents.

These publications perform a valuable service in providing relatively
current data, compared to what could have been offered in a publication
issued previously without supplements. Although not as current as
periodicals, they are more so than handbooks, encyclopedias, and the
like.

Annuals and yearbooks differ from each other in the variety of subject
matter they present. In addition, they may have either commercial or
not-for-profit sponsorship; they may be part of another publication (such
as a special issue offered without charge to a periodical), or may be for
sale only as a separate title; and they may cumulate some of the data from

previous editions (such as is done in *Statistical Abstracts*) or they may have only new data. Their scope may be all-encompassing, such as the annual yearbooks issued to update the *McGraw-Hill Encyclopedia of Science and Technology,* or it may be as narrow as the annual volume updating a bibliography on refrigeration.

The following examples constitute merely a small sample of the types of works making up this class of publications.

Aerospace Industries Association of America. *Aerospace Facts and Figures.* Fallbrook, Calif.: 1945-   . Annual.

>   Presents statistics of a wide scope pertaining to the aerospace industry.

Jane's Fighting Ships. New York: McGraw-Hill, 1897-   . Annual.

>   A well-illustrated yearly directory of ships in various navies. Includes related topics, such as submarines, missiles, and aircraft (naval). Has an index arranged by ship or project name.

McGraw-Hill Yearbook of Science and Technology. New York: McGraw-Hill, 1962-   . Annual.

>   Updates the *McGraw-Hill Encyclopedia of Science and Technology.* The largest section contains alphabetically arranged articles on developments during the past year. A second section presents outstanding scientific photographs of the year, while a third section consists of several articles discussing subjects of growing interest.

>   (*See also* Directories)

Annual Reviews

At least in the beginning of its history, this type of literature reviewed the annual progress in a discipline and presented highlights of the year. Now some are merely collections of good, lengthy, well-documented material worthy of a scholarly journal but do not really furnish the annual summary they once featured.

They are offered under at least three main series titles, beginning with one of these three phrases: *Progress in . . . ,* or, *Advances in . . . ,* or, *Annual Review of . . . .* Their scope may be as narrow as automatic programming or as broad as nuclear physics. They keep proliferating, with more and more narrow topics being chosen as the subject for yet another review series. If a library collects in the area involved, it is difficult to ignore them since they do generally offer material of research value. However, budgets strained by rising costs of existing periodicals and serials make librarians less than enthusiastic to learn of yet another title in these series.

One other problem is that of retrieving material listed within them. Many indexing and abstracting services do not index their articles; some are in a gray area where they are not covered by any well-known index. This is unfortunate, since their contents are often very good. Their articles often feature numerous literature references to a given topic, which, when done by the specialists usually chosen to write the articles, are quite valuable. However, the recent index listed below may allieviate this problem.

Index to Scientific Reviews. Philadelphia: Institute for Scientific Information, 1975- . Semiannual.

Indexes review articles from over 2,700 journals and annual review publications. Cumulates annually. Allows for searching by authors, title words, and organizations, along with a citation index.

The following lists, while showing only a portion of the many annual review series in existence, should suffice to indicate the variety of subjects covered by this type of literature. Only the titles and publishers are shown.

Advances in . . . . Series

Analytical Chemistry and Instrumentation (Wiley)
Applied Mechanics (Academic)
Applied Microbiology (Academic)
Astronomy and Astrophysics (Academic)
Biochemical Engineering (Springer-Verlag)
Biomedical Engineering and Medical Physics (Wiley)

Botanical Research (Academic)
Chemical Engineering (Academic)
Chromatography (Dekker)
Computers (Academic)
Control Systems (Academic)
Cryogenic Engineering (Plenum)
Ecological Research (Academic)
Electrochemistry and Electrochemical Engineering (Wiley)
Electronics and Electron Physics (Academic)
Environmental Sciences (Wiley)
Genetics (Academic)
Geophysics (Academic)
Hydroscience (Academic)
Machine Tool Design and Research (Pergamon)
Marine Biology (Academic)
Materials Research (Wiley)
Microwaves (Academic)
Nuclear Science and Technology (Academic)
Organic Chemistry (Wiley)
Petroleum Chemistry and Refining (Wiley)
Plasma Physics (Wiley)
Polymer Science (Springer-Verlag)
Probability (Dekker)
Space Science and Technology (Academic)
Vacuum Science and Technology (Pergamon)
Water Pollution Research (Pergamon)
X-Ray Analysis (Plenum)

Annual Review of . . . . Series

Automatic Programming (Pergamon)
Fluid Mechanics (Annual Reviews, Inc.)
Genetics (Annual Reviews, Inc.)
Materials Science (Annual Reviews, Inc.)
NMR Spectroscopy (Academic)
Nuclear Science (Annual Reviews, Inc.)
Physical Chemistry (Annual Reviews, Inc.)
Psychology (Annual Reviews, Inc.)

Progress in . . . . Series

Aeronautical Sciences (Pergamon)
Applied Materials Research (Gordon)
Biophysics and Molecular Biology (Pergamon)
Ceramic Science (Pergamon)
Cryogenics (Academic)
Dielectrics (Academic)
Heat and Mass Transfer (Pergamon)
High Temperature Physics and Chemistry (Pergamon)
Oceanography (Pergamon)
Polymer Science (Pergamon)
Quantum Electronics (Pergamon)
Semiconductors (Wiley)
Solid Mechanics (American Elsevier)
Surface Science (Pergamon)

Other Types of Literature

This section will be concerned with a variety of types of materials, including technical reports, patents, directories, standards, and audiovisual materials.

Technical Reports

These are comparatively short monographic works prepared by or for agencies whose funding does not depend on sale of the reports. The subjects of the reports are usually quite specific and are written primarily for a select group of readers. It is incidental that most technical reports are softbound (in the original). They are prepared chiefly for government agencies or commercial sponsors. More often than not their subjects appeal more to engineers or applied scientists than to pure scientists. Their identification is chiefly by one or more unique report numbers assigned to them, often part of a series.

Tens of thousands of reports are issued each year by the three main U.S. government agencies responsible for the bulk of the federal technical report literature—namely, NASA, the Energy Research and Development Agency (formerly the Atomic Energy Commission), and the Department of Commerce's National Technical Information

Agency (NTIS). Thousands of reports also emanate from smaller agencies, such as the Bureau of Mines and the Geological Survey.

Scientists in some disciplines, such as theoretical physics, may have little or no interest in technical reports, although those interested in applied nuclear physics have a keen interest in ERDA reports. The same relationship holds for theoretical chemists versus those interested in nuclear chemistry. Engineers generally have the most use for technical reports, compared to their colleagues in scientific disciplines.

Technical reports are written primarily for people involved in the subject at hand, and they are not intended to serve a tutorial purpose. Those appearing as project reports on a given contract are even less meaningful to readers unacquainted with the project for which they were written.

Agencies such as the NTIS have been established to expedite the sale of reports and to provide reference assistance on technical reports for the general public. Contractors for the government can usually go to their sponsoring agency for assistance in obtaining copies and/or other assistance. Another source is the regional report collections maintained by universities or state libraries. In many cases they will loan reports to any requester and offer assistance in identifying reports and the like.

As in the case of periodicals, the sci-tech world would be greatly handicapped if there were no indexing and abstracting services for technical reports. Fortunately, they do exist, and some are excellent, while others are merely fair.

The best indexing services are those which have not only indexes for personal authors and subjects but also for contract numbers, report numbers, and names of agencies involved in report preparation. They are usually computer-printed, with cumulations at least each year. Annotations, available in all but the most mediocre indexes, tend to be indicative. Subject headings vary among the various government indexing services; efforts at standardization have not succeeded to date.

A very useful index provided by the ERDA is a cumulative one arranged by report number. It has the unusual feature of listing the published literature that may have been prepared to match given report numbers. This allows a person to find equivalent monographic or periodical material if the report version is not available. It may not be an exact equivalent but is still worth knowing about.

Report Indexing and Abstracting Services

Science and Engineering (General)

Government Reports Announcements. Springfield, Va.: U.S. National Technical Information Service, 1971- . Semimonthly.

Covers a wide range of report literature, as it indexes scientific, technical, business, and economic data written by or for government agencies, including the Department of Defense. All items have both an annotation and a listing of subject headings or descriptors. Continues the scope and coverage of *U.S. Government Research and Development Reports,* which it supersedes. Its indexes are now issued in *Government Reports Index* (which see).

Government Reports Index. Springfield, Va.: U.S. National Technical Information Service, 1971- . Semimonthly.

Serves as an index to *Government Reports Announcements* (which see). Each issue has separate indexes for subjects, personal authors, agency sources (corporate authors), contract numbers, and report numbers, all cumulating annually. Continues the index portion of *U.S. Government Research and Development Reports* which it supersedes.

Aeronautics and Astronautics

Scientific and Technical Aerospace Reports. College Park, Md.: U.S. National Aeronautics and Space Administration, 1963- . Semimonthly.

Covers both aeronautics and astronautics, with scientific and technical data both represented, as far as technical reports are concerned. (For a coverage of books and journals, see *International Aerospace Abstracts.*) Indexes in each issue cover authors, sponsoring agencies, subjects, report numbers, and contract numbers, with indexes cumulated on a semiannual and annual basis.

Nuclear Science

Nuclear Science Abstracts. Oak Ridge, Tenn.: U.S. Energy Research and Development Administration, 1948-   . Semimonthly.

Includes not only reports but also books, journals, patents, etc., with all items annotated. Has separate indexes for subjects, personal authors, agency sources (corporate authors), and report numbers. Its indexes cumulate quarterly and annually; some cover even longer periods.

Report Codes

Special Libraries Association. *Dictionary of Report Series Codes.* 2d ed. Edited by Lois E. Godfrey and Helen F. Redman. New York, 1973. 645 p.

Provides an index to codes used to identify technical report services. One index is arranged by code versus identifying source, while the other is by source with the accompanying code. A useful tool for identifying reports.

Patents

Although the importance of patents to the business and industrial world is well accepted, as types of literature they have a rather minor role to play at university sci-tech libraries. Perhaps the lack of commercial interest in developing products or creating marketable new ones accounts for the low interest in patents on campuses. Exclusion of patents from a university collection presents no problem, however. The *Gazettes* issued by the U.S. Patent Office—one for patents and one for trademarks—and its indexes should suffice in most cases. If a university is near a large public library which keeps patents, there is no need to keep either the patents or the *Gazette.*

Several periodical indexing and abstracting services, such as *Chemical Abstracts,* regularly index not only U.S. chemical patents but foreign ones as well. Commercial indexes are available for particular types of patents, such as for electronic devices and petroleum products.

U.S. Patent Office. *Manual of Classification.* Washington, D.C.: Superintendent of Documents.

> Consists of a looseleaf volume, available on a subscription basis for supplements, which lists the numbers and titles of the more than three hundred main classes and the sixty-six thousand subclasses used in the subject classification of patents.

U.S. Patent Office. *Official Gazette: Patents.* Washington, D.C.: Superintendent of Documents, 1971-   . Weekly.

> Lists recently issued patents, showing a selected diagram, a brief abstract of the text, name of patentee, etc. Has an annual index of patentees and of subjects. A continuation of the serial which began in 1872.

U.S. Patent Office. *Official Gazette: Trademarks.* Washington, D.C.: Superintendent of Documents, 1971-   . Weekly.

> Indexes recently issued trademarks. Gives an illustration of the trademark. Has an annual index. A continuation of the serial which began in 1872.

Directories

The many types of directories available make them popular in most libraries, and sci-tech units are no exception. They range from those devoted to biography to others specializing in companies selling a particular product, such as electronic equipment. Many are issued annually, while others are issued irregularly. Some are quite limited in scope, while others cover a wide range. This section will discuss some of the more important types of directories.

Biographical Directories—This section includes not only the widely known, broadly based *Who's Who in America* but specific directories for workers in a particular field, such as computer and data processing personnel, or outstanding engineers.

A broad, all-encompassing directory of engineers has not been published in recent years. This represents a real gap in the literature. One substitute, or backup for existing directories, as the case may be, is the annual directory of members issued by most societies. They rarely tell more than the bare minimum about each person, and they are not selective, but a times they meet a real need.

Manufacturers' Directories—One of the most common needs is to locate the names and addresses, sometimes the products, of manufacturing companies. The most widely known one is *Thomas' Register,* which has a products index with thousands of entries plus special features mentioned below. Other directories are limited to a certain field, such as the annual buyers' guide published by *Electronics* magazine. Another type of manufacturers' directory is sponsored by an agency in a state government, listing only companies located within that state. This information needs regular updating.

Other Directories—Directories of laboratories are similar to those of manufacturers but are limited to those companies that maintain research laboratories. Such directories fill many a need, whether it be that of the graduate student looking for employment or that of the businessman looking for a company to act as consultant for a specialized technical problem.

Other types of directories include those for educational and scientific organizations, which itemize their publications and activities.

Biographical Directories

American Men and Women of Science. Physical and Biological Sciences Section. 12th ed. Ann Arbor, Mich.: Bowker, 1971-1973. 6 vols.

Contains over 145,000 biographies, covering six hundred areas of science. Data presented include subject interests and society memberships. Provides separate necrology. The social and behavioral sciences are covered in a companion set of volumes.

Dictionary of Scientific Biography. Edited by C. G. Gillispie. New York: Scribners, 1970-   . Issued irregularly.

A compilation which will consist of twelve volumes (and have five thousand entries) plus an index volume when completed. Co-sponsored by the National Science Foundation and the American Council of Learned Societies. Excludes living scientists and extends back to antiquity. Nine volumes published by 1974.

Engineers of Distinction: A Who's Who in Engineering. 2d ed. New York: Engineers Joint Council, 1973. 401 p.

Restricted to living engineers who have won distinction in industry, education, government, or professional circles. Lists around five thousand engineers.

Ireland, Norma. *Index to Scientists of the World from Ancient to Modern Times: Biographies and Portraits.* Westwood, Mass.: Faxon, 1962. 662 p.

Lists over four hundred publications which cover more than seventy-four hundred different scientists. Includes portraits as well as biographical works.

McGraw-Hill Modern Men of Science. New York: McGraw-Hill, 1966-1968. 2 vols.

A selection limited to less than one thousand invited persons. Each entry includes a sketch of the scientist as well as a description of career highlights. Has a name and a subject index.

Who's Who in Engineering. 9th ed. New York: Lewis Historical Publishing Co., 1964. 2,198 p.

Still a good source for data on thousands of engineers, although it is out of print. Limited to those with fifteen years of experience. Supplies standard biographical information.

Who's Who in Science in Europe. A Reference Guide to European Scientists. 2d ed. Guernsey, British Isles: Hodgson, 1972. 4 vols.

Covers nearly forty thousand entries and cross references. Includes scientists from East Europe as well as West European countries.

World Who's Who in Science: A Biographical Dictionary of Notable Scientists from Antiquity to the Present. Chicago: Marquis, 1968. 1,855 p.

Lists around thirty thousand sketches of prominent scientists, nearly half of whom are no longer living. Includes a description of their contributions.

Manufacturers' Directories

Best's Safety Directory: Safety, Industrial Hygiene, Security. Oldwick, N.J.:A. M. Best Co., 1946-   . Biennial.

A directory of manufacturers of safety and pollution control equipment. Includes fire protection, industrial hygiene, machinery guards, plant maintenance, transportation safety, air and water pollution controls, and security material. The fifteenth edition was published in 1975.

Chemical Engineering Catalog: The Process Industries Catalog. New York: Van Nostrand Reinhold, 1916-   . Annual.

A collection of manufacturers' catalogs concerned with processing equipment and related materials. Organized by company. Has indexes by product and by trade names also. In its fifty-eighth year in 1974.

Electronic Buyers' Guide. New York: McGraw-Hill, 1946-   . Annual.

Includes manufacturers' addresses and a product arrangement of vendors.

Sweet's Catalog File. New York: McGraw-Hill Information Systems Co., 1914-   . Annual.

Consists of collections of manufacturers' catalogs, centered around certain products, such as architectural materials, machine tools, and plant engineering.

World Mines Register. San Francisco: Miller Freeman, 1974- .
Annual.

Supersedes *Mines Register.* Lists operating mines (arranged by
type of process or material), an alphabetical and a geographic list of
companies, and a directory of nearly ten thousand persons. Covers
over eighty countries.

(*See also* Manufacturers' catalogs)

Other Directories

American Chemical Society. *Directory of Graduate Research.*
Washington, D.C.: the Society, 1953- . Biennial.

Describes faculty research at universities in the United States and
Canada offering doctorates in chemistry, chemical engineering,
biochemistry, and pharmaceutical or medicinal chemistry. Lists the
latest publications of the faculty members and their fields of
research.

Cass, James; Max Birnbaum, eds. *Comparative Guide to Science
and Engineering Programs.* New York: Harper & Row, 1971. 1,
165 p.

Provides an account of the programs offered by selected colleges
and universities in the sciences and engineering, covering twenty-
five hundred departments. Describes size of faculty, courses
offered, grade requirements, graduate study outlook, etc. Statistics
on enrollment, arranged by school, are given.

Directory of Engineering Societies and Related Organizations. 7th
ed. New York: Engineers Joint Council, 1974. 178 p. (Supplement issued in 1972).

Presents data on three hundred national, regional, and international organizations involved with engineering.

Encyclopedia of Information Systems and Services. International edition. Edited by Anthony T. Kruzas. Ann Arbor, Mich.: Edwards Brothers, 1974. 1,271 p.

A directory to seventeen hundred fifty organizations concerned with information products and services, including data base publishers (nearly five hundred of them), research centers and projects, networks and cooperative programs, and government information sources.

Industrial Research Laboratories of the United States. 14th ed. New York: Bowker, 1975. 585 p.

Lists over sixty-six hundred laboratories within over three thousand companies. Gives name of company, personnel and subject fields, etc. Has a subject index, a personnel index, and a geographical index.

Scientific, Technical and Engineering Societies Publications in Print 1974-1975. Edited by James M. Kyed and James M. Matarazzo. New York: Bowker, 1974. 223 p.

Provides bibliographic data on publications (periodicals, books, symposia, newsletters, audiovisual material, etc.), for over one hundred fifty technical and scientific societies. Includes keyword and author/editor indexes.

Scientific, Technical and Related Societies of the United States. 9th ed. Washington, D.C.: National Academy of Sciences, 1971. 213 p.

Lists over five hundred societies, giving a description of size, location of headquarters, publications, fields of interest, etc. Has a subject index.

World Directory of Environmental Research Centers. 2d ed. Edited by William K. Wilson and others. New York: Bowker, 1974. 448 p.

Lists around fifty-three hundred organizations included in environmental research in over one hundred countries. Gives details on staff size and activities, both governmental and private.

World Guide to Scientific Associations. New York: Bowker, 1974. 481 p.

Lists over ten thousand associations (from one hundred thirty-four countries) involved in science and research. Arranged geographically, then alphabetically by title. Includes a detailed subject index.

Proceedings of Meetings

This type of literature is variously known as proceedings, transactions, or conference records. They all pertain to publications that contain copies of papers (or synopses thereof) given at technical meetings, whether they be called conferences, conventions, symposia, or similar names. Hundreds of high caliber meetings take place throughout the year. Since only a small percentage of interested scientists or engineers can attend the average conference, the only alternative is to try to obtain a copy of papers given there, sometimes in the form of a bound set obtained from the sponsoring agency.

Some are issued in advance of a meeting (in which case they are rarely more than synopses, each of several hundred words in length); others appear later, perhaps in hardback book form, issued more than a year or two following a meeting. As will be noted, there is a useful index available covering meetings having proceedings, as well as indexes to meetings regardless of the question of proceedings.

One reason why proceedings are important in sci-tech libraries is that the papers usually represent advanced reports of developments, sometimes appearing in that form for the first time. Other papers are available only in the proceedings of the meetings at which given, having never been resubmitted to journal editors for publication.

Directory of Published Proceedings. Series SEMT. Harrison, N.Y.: InterDok Corp., 1964-   . 10 issues per year.

Each issue has a subject/sponsor index, a location index, all of which cumulate annually along with cumulative chronological listings. Confined to science-engineering material.

Proceedings in Print. Mattapan, Mass.: 1964-   . Bimonthly.

Indexes published conference proceedings in all languages and in all subjects. Listings are alphabetical by keyword of conference title. Also lists those meetings for which proceedings will not be published. Each issue also has an index of sponsors. Indexes cumulate annually.

Standards and Specifications

This type of literature is generally of more interest to engineers and possibly to some applied scientists than to pure scientists. Standards, which are so similar to specifications that they will be regarded as synonymous here, are primarily documents giving detailed instructions for approved methods of making a particular product, or performing a certain process, or the like. They are indispensable as safeguards of life and property in many cases, such as the construction of safe highways, properly designed electrical goods, or pure and harmless food products. Other standards promote economy and efficiency, including standards for screw threads, light bulbs, or filing cabinets.

The U.S. government is the most prolific publisher of standards, many of which are for military products and others for civilian government uses. Indexes exist for both types, making the task of identifying them easier.

Some standards, prepared by technical and scientific societies, feature materials and products pertinent to their field of activity. The main source in the United States for general specifications covering a wide scope is the American National Standards Institute, a nongovernmental and not-for-profit agency which develops original standards as well as sponsors those previously accepted by scientific and engineering societies before submission to ANSI. It has close ties with international standards agencies as well as U.S. groups.

Standards are carefully marked as to their date of acceptance. Users need to be sure they are using the latest edition since the content can and does change radically from one edition to the next.

Many are so technical in nature that only experienced people can hope to understand them or use them; others, depending upon the subject matter, are written for a wider audience.

American National Standards Institute. *Catalog*. New York: 1950(?)-   .
    Annual.

Its standards cover all areas of technology and related fields, and are known unofficially as "national" standards. Also lists certain international standards. Has a detailed subject index.

U.S. Department of Defense. *Index of Specifications and Standards.* Washington, D.C.: 1951-. Bimonthly.

Lists all unclassified specifications and standards adopted by the Department of Defense. Has one volume arranged alphabetically by title, one by a classification system, and one by the standard numbers. Indicates availability, number, and date of latest edition, etc. Has an annual cumulation.

U.S. General Services Administration. *Index of Federal Specifications and Standards.* Washington, D.C.: Superintendent of Documents, 1952-. Monthly.

Indexes nonmilitary specifications accepted for federal use. Arranged by subject classification, by number, and alphabetically by title. Includes prices, date, edition numbers. Has an annual cumulation.

Manufacturers' Catalogs

Brochures and catalogs from manufacturers, sometimes called trade catalogs, at best serve a fringe area in sci-tech libraries at universities. They are much more important in the collections of special libraries in industry and business, where materials and equipment are bought on a wider scale than on the campuses.

However, a given laboratory in a department of instruction, or the manager of a machine shop serving physicists, or university purchasing departments are examples of groups who use trade catalogs regularly. Even librarians need to keep catalogs of sources of library equipment and furniture.

One new development in recent years has been the inclusion of trade catalogs from those manufacturers wishing to do so in separate volumes of *Thomas Register*. At one time catalogs were available on microfilm as well as on microfiche, but the continuity of such sets has not been steady. Buyers' guides have often included large advertisements for manufacturers, perhaps even for catalog pages, but again this has not been a reliable source.

It is doubtful that any sci-tech library at a university should ever get involved in keeping trade catalogs for its users. The exception would be if the unit served had such well-focused needs that a collection to suit its needs would not be overwhelmingly large. Having a collection of trade catalogs involves obtaining new editions annually, which is often a time-consuming process.

Thomas Register of American Manufacturers and Thomas Register Catalog File. New York: Thomas Publishing Co., 1905- . Annual.

> Serves as a comprehensive directory of thousands of American manufacturing companies. Has a product arrangement as well as separate lists of company addresses, brand names, and trademarks. Also separate volumes now exist which present reproductions of companies' trade catalogs. The 1974 set, its sixty-fourth edition, had eleven volumes.

Zimmerman, O. T.; I. Lavine, eds. *Handbook of Industrial Trade Names.* Dover, N.H.: Industrial Research Service, 1953-1965. 1 volume and 4 supplements.

> Provides an alphabetical listing of trade names. An index arranged by type of use is included, along with a directory of manufacturers involved.

(*See also* Manufacturers' Directories)

Translations

In addition to cover-to-cover translations, libraries sometimes need translations of articles or books. As the listing here shows, a national depository maintained in Chicago (at the John Crerar Library) has its own index. The modest price for items is much lower than the cost of having items translated. It has recently been estimated that translations of articles cost at least $4 to $5 per one hundred English words. This can be costly for an article or book portion several pages long.

Several government agencies issue translation series; one of the best known is NASA's. Work is done on a contract in most cases, and the quality appears to be consistently good.

Once obtained, translations are probably best cataloged. This is a convenience to users who will find them more easily this way than if they were merely put in vertical files or other ephemeral collections.

Himmelsbach, Carl J; Grace E. Brociner. *A Guide to Scientific and Technical Journals in Translation.* 2d ed. New York: Special Libraries Association, 1972. 49 p.

> Lists mostly cover-to-cover translations into English of foreign language periodicals. Both translated and original titles are included.

Translation Register-Index. Chicago: National Translations Center, John Crerar Library, 1967-   . Semimonthly.

> Presents an index to translations available at a nominal fee from the center. Each issue has patent and journal citation indexes, which cumulate quarterly and annually. Continues previous indexes having various titles, including those when the project was operated by the Special Libraries Association.

Maps

Many universities have a central map collection in which can be found a variety of types, such as geological, historical, economic, as well as those of just geographical interest. At other universities the geological maps are kept in the geology library or as part of a centralized science library.

These maps should be cataloged unless they are in series for which one can rely on indexes prepared by issuing sources. Entries by geographical area covered are preferable to those by source or cartographer.

The U.S. Geological Survey issues thousands of maps covering small areas. This is part of a national program to prepare up-to-date topographic maps of the U.S. Military agencies, such as the Defense Mapping Agency and the Air Force, are prolific sources of fine, detailed maps on a global basis. Commercial and not-for-profit agencies also issue good maps, but on a smaller level than the government agencies.

Sales catalogs for dealers specializing in maps, both current and out-of-print, are valuable assets in trying to locate particular maps. Another useful source is the index to maps which has been recently published per the item in the listing below.

Atlases are needed in several sci-tech libraries since almost every unit should have a good general purpose atlas on hand. Specialized ones could also be kept in one unit, such as with the geological maps. But for professors going on trips, or for purposes of locating the sites of international conferences or for other related purposes, an up-to-date atlas is needed in each library.

International Maps and Atlases in Print. Compiled by K. L. Winch. New York: Bowker, 1974. 862 p.

> Gives a description of over eight thousand maps and atlases, including full details as to title, scale, series number, editor, size, and source of publication. Arranged geographically. Ranges from star charts to railway maps.

Special Libraries Association. Geography and Map Division. Directory Revision Committee. *Map Collections in the United States and Canada.* Edited by David K. Carrington. New York, 1970. 159 p.

> Gives a description of the size and type of map collections in over six hundred institutions. Institutions are arranged alphabetically by city within a state or province. Subject specialization is indicated.

Thesauri

Closely akin to dictionaries are thesauri—sets of accepted terms used in indexing services for periodicals and/or technical reports. The scientific and technical compilations are often very elaborate, with cross references to related terms and references from terms not used to accepted terms.

One of the broadest thesauri is that issued by the Engineers Joint Council. It covers all aspects of engineering and related fields.

One advantage of thesauri is that they enable one to locate the best term to use in a search if casual use of an indexing service volume is not productive. Although they do, of course, go out of date easily, they serve a useful purpose.

Engineers Joint Council. *Thesaurus of Engineering and Scientific Terms.* New York, 1967. 690 p.

A work best described by the subtitle: "A list of engineering and related scientific terms and their relationships for use as a vocabulary reference in indexing and retrieving technical information." Besides the main alphabetical approach, it also has a keyword index, an index by twenty-two COSATI fields, and an index showing the descriptors arranged by family relationships.

Psychology

Kinkade, Robert G., ed. *A Thesaurus of Psychological Index Terms.* Washington, D.C.: American Psychological Association, 1974. 362 p.

Contains about four thousand terms of primary importance to psychology. Its three indexes will list terms by hierarchy, alphabetically, and by relationships to other terms.

Histories

There is a body of literature devoted to the history of science and/or technology. Some journals are devoted entirely to this subject, while multivolumed reference sets exist which give detailed accounts of this nature. In addition, there are separate monographs and even periodical articles on the subject.

Writers should match the subject at hand with the length of publication involved. A history of science in general would require a large volume at least, with multivolumed sets more appropriate. Yet a history of one small topic, such as gas lasers or analogue computers, could be reasonably well handled in a periodical article.

Historical accounts furnish readers with good perspective which cannot easily be obtained from current literature alone.

Chemistry

Partington, J. R. *A History of Chemistry.* New York: St. Martin's Press, 1961-1970. 4 vols.

A thorough work, covering the subject from early Greek philosophy into the twentieth century. Done in a careful, scholarly fashion.

Civil Engineering

Straub, Hans. *History of Civil Engineering: An Outline from Ancient to Modern Times*. Cambridge, Mass.: MIT Press, 1952. 258 p.

Covers a time period of thousands of years and discusses techniques and problems encountered in each era. Separate indexes for subjects, personal names, and place names are provided in this well-illustrated volume.

Electronics

Shiers, George. *Bibliography of the History of Electronics*. Metuchen, N.J.: Scarecrow, 1972. 323 p.

Covers the historical aspects of electronics and telecommunication. Contains over eighteen hundred items in classed order.

Engineering (General)

Ferguson, Eugene S., ed. *Bibliography of the History of Technology*. Cambridge, Mass.: MIT Press, 1968. 347 p.

Presents an impressive annotated compilation of works arranged in broad subject categories (mechanical engineering, materials and processes, etc.), as well as by divisions such as biography and manuscripts. Literature which contains bibliographies is emphasized. Has an author index.

Rapport, Samuel; Helen Wright, eds. *Engineering*. New York: New York University Press, 1963. 378 p.

Offers a collection of essays covering the period from ancient times to the present. Ranges from a discussion of da Vinci's works to the uses of atomic energy. An interesting compilation.

Mathematics

May, Kenneth O. *Bibliography and Research Manual of the History of Mathematics.* Toronto: University of Toronto Press, 1973. 818 p.

Contains about thirty-one thousand entries, arranged by subject, or by historical time periods or by persons. Includes a list of about three thousand periodical titles of interest, arranged by their abbreviations.

Metallurgy

Dennis, William H. *A Hundred Years of Metallurgy.* Chicago: Aldine Publishing Co., 1963. 342 p.

Has nine chapters, arranged by types of metals or by processes. Each chapter covers a wide time period. Has name and subject indexes.

Psychology

Roback, A. A. *History of Psychology and Psychiatry.* New York: Philosophical Library, 1961. 422 p.

Has six sections, one of which consists of biographies of eminent people in the field, ranging from Aristotle to the present. Other personages are described, arranged by national origin. The largest section describes events and people in abnormal and medical psychology. Other sections deal with other branches of the subject.

Preprints

In many areas of science the preprint is very important. The term here is defined as any copy of a publication available before its intended publication has taken place. The usual format is that of unpublished periodical articles.

Physicists probably rely on preprints, particularly in the field of high energy physics, as much as any other type of scientist. One reason is the great speed with which new findings and theories can be distributed by means of preprints. Rather than waiting months for the journal articles to appear, distribution of preprints saves much time for those fortunate enough to have them.

There is little organized in this field, although the listing below shows one index for preprints is available.

Preprints in Particles and Fields. Stanford, Calif.: Stanford Linear Accelerator Center Library. Weekly.

Lists new high-energy physics preprints received at the SLAC Library. Lists preprints by author, title, and number, characterized as to whether they emphasize experimentation, theory, instruments, computations, or a review of work.

Dissertations and Master's Theses

Doctoral dissertations are at the forefront of research inasmuch as the topics must be original. Furthermore, they are unbiased and well monitored, because of the thoroughness with which doctoral candidates are queried by their examiners. With the advent of the microfilmed set of dissertations by University Microfilms, the present owner of the files, the United States began to get these rather elusive materials under good bibliographic control. Virtually all major universities now participate in this program, and indexes are becoming more and more useful. One comprehensive bibliography, listed below, is truly a great step forward bibliographically. A high percentage of the back files and current dissertations involve science or engineering.

Master's theses have less standing academically and intellectually than dissertations because they take less time to prepare, are done by students less advanced than doctoral candidates, and have less bibliographic control. Only one index, listed below, has much significance for the retrieval or identification of these documents. More and more departments of instruction are eliminating the requirement of a master's thesis, so the number issued each year should be lessening.

American Doctoral Dissertations. Ann Arbor, Mich.: University Microfilms, 1955/1956- . Annual.

Offers a listing of all doctoral dissertations accepted by United

States and Canadian universities. As a result, this list includes many which are not found in *Dissertation Abstracts International*. Arranged by appropriate subjects, then by institution. Has an author index.

Comprehensive Dissertation Index, 1861-1972. Ann Arbor, Mich.: University Microfilms, 1973. 37 vols.

Lists over four hundred thousand dissertations, grouped by discipline, then alphabetically by keywords. Indexes include authors and keywords in the titles. Volumes on specific disciplines are available separately. This monumental set should be a valuable tool.

Dissertation Abstracts International. Part B—The Sciences and Engineering. Ann Arbor, Mich.: University Microfilms, 1938-   . Monthly.

Indexes doctoral dissertations submitted for microfilming by over 250 United States and Canadian universities. Uses subject categories, such as geology and physics, for its arrangement, and includes detailed abstracts. Each issue has a keyword title index and an author index, with the latter cumulated annually.

Purdue University. Thermophysical Properties Center. *Masters Theses in the Pure and Applied Sciences Accepted by Colleges and Universities of the United States.* West Lafayette, Ind.: Ann Arbor, Mich.: University Microfilms, 1957-   . Annual.

Commencing with the thesis year of 1955, lists the master's theses from over two hundred United States universities and colleges. Organized by subject categories, such as electrical engineering and physics.

Tables

Data presented in tabular form are of great value to science and engineering, as these disciplines rely on known data that can be concisely stated. Tabular material does, of course, become outdated, but revisions are relatively easy. The advent of computer-printed tables is making the updating of tables less expensive and more accurate. Hopefully, then, printed tables will be more abundant in the future and more frequently revised than in the past.

Tables can cover a very wide scope, such as data on all aspects of chemistry and physics, or they can be devoted to one narrow topic, e.g., logarithms or optical properties of semiconductors. Whatever their nature, they deserve careful attention and have a rightful place in the reference collection.

Biochemistry

CRC Handbook of Biochemistry: Selected Data for Molecular Biology. 2d ed. Edited by Herbert A. Sober. Cleveland, Ohio: Chemical Rubber Co., 1970. Variously paged.

> Has sections devoted to topics typified by amino acids, carbohydrates, genetics and biology, nucleic acids, etc. Most sections are essentially tabular.

Chemistry

Handbook of Chemistry and Physics. Cleveland, Ohio: Chemical Rubber Co., 1913-   . Annual.

> A widely used, valuable reference source. Offers thousands of tables giving basic physical and chemical data, plus conversion factors, mathematical tables, chemical structures, etc.

Lange's Handbook of Chemistry. 11th ed. Compiled by John A. Dean. New York: McGraw-Hill, 1973. Variously paged.

> Almost entirely in tabular form, listing properties of chemical substances grouped into such topics as organic chemistry, spectroscopy, and electrochemistry. A comprehensive set of tables.

Engineering

CRC Handbook of Tables for Applied Engineering Science. 2d ed.

Edited by Ray E. Bolz. Cleveland, Ohio: CRC Press, 1973. 1,150 p.

Has eleven chapters, which deal with engineering materials and various types of engineering (electrical, chemical, nuclear, energy, and mechanical) as well as the human environment, safety, computation, measurements, etc. Provides practicing engineers with a wide spectrum of data. Uses SI units as well as conventional units.

Mathematics

Burington, Richard S., comp. *Handbook of Mathematical Tables and Formulas.* 5th ed. New York: McGraw-Hill, 1973. 500 p.

Features basic tables (trigonometry, integrals, logarithms, powers, etc.) as well as those related to finance (interest and actuarial tables) and similar material. Definitions and theorems are also included.

CRC Standard Mathematical Tables. 22d ed. Edited by Samuel M. Selby. Cleveland, Ohio: CRC Press, 1974. 708 p.

Has now added use of the metric system to the material on measurements. Mensuration, circular and hyperbolic trigonometry, analytical geometry, algebra of sets, determinants and matrices, integral tables, Laplace and Fourier transforms, and vector analysis are representative topics.

Handbook of Tables for Mathematics. 4th ed. Edited by Robert C. Weast. Cleveland, Ohio: Chemical Rubber Co., 1970. 1,120 p.

Tables arranged in groups such as logarithms, matrices and determinants, trigonometry, differential equations, probability. Hundreds of tables are given.

Handbook of Tables for Probability and Statistics. Edited by W. H. Beyer. Cleveland, Ohio: Chemical Rubber Co., 1966. 502 p.

Involves probability, various distributions (normal, binomial, Poisson, Chi-square, etc.), range, quality control, correlation coefficients, and related topics.

Metals

Smithells, Colin J., ed. *Metals Reference Book.* 4th ed. Washington, D.C.: IFI Plenum, 1967. 3 vols.

Presents tabular data on all aspects of metals, including diffusion in metals, crystallography, properties (physical, electrical, and mechanical), casting, welding.

Woldman, Norman E., ed. *Engineering Alloys.* 5th ed. New York: Van Nostrand Reinhold, 1973. 1,440 p.

One listing of alloys is by serial number, giving trade name, composition, properties, and uses. The second listing is alphabetical by trade names and corresponding serial numbers. Also included are indexes by manufacturer and certain tabular data. Nearly fifteen thousand new alloys have been added since the previous edition in 1962.

Minerals

U.S. Bureau of Mines. *Minerals Yearbook.* Washington, D.C.: Superintendent of Documents, 1933-   . Annual.

Reviews the world's minerals industry. Its volumes are devoted to metals, minerals and fuels; area reports (domestic); and area reports (international). Prices, production, consumption, etc., are tabulated.

Physics

Kaye, George W.; T. H. Laby, eds. *Tables of Physical and Chemical Constants and Some Mathematical Functions.* 13th ed. New York: Wiley, 1966. 249 p.

Involves general physics, chemistry, mathematics, and atomic physics. There is only a small amount of text and formulas.

Smithsonian Physical Tables. 9th rev. ed. Compiled by William E. Forsythe. Washington, D.C.: Smithsonian Institution, 1964. 827 p. (Publication #4169).

Has nine hundred tables covering a wide scope of physical properties. Includes, for instance, atomic data, many tables on heat, optical properties, properties of gases and fluids, atmospheric data.

Audiovisual Aids

There is a growing body of A/V material on the sciences and engineering, although to date the medical field has taken the lead in this regard. However, films, audio and video recordings, slides, and filmstrips exist on topics of interest to many scientists and engineers. Their primary value at this time seems to be for instructional purposes. A lecture on video tape, produced in a department's own classroom, can be used over and over, benefiting students who were absent or those who need a repetition in order to master the material. The same can be said of motion pictures, whether to illustrate some involved experiment or phenomena. Repetition is no problem when it is on film.

Some publications are being issued only in cassette format, whether they be proceedings of a conference, supplementary material, or current awareness lectures for keeping scientists and engineers up to date. Societies have been active in these fields at the collegiate level; commercial firms seem to have concentrated more on elementary and secondary education.

Libraries that need such materials will find them more expensive than monographs. Reproduction equipment of good quality is also costly. However, many librarians believe this area has great future growth, particularly for instructional purposes.

At present there are no recommended indexes to collegiate-level sci-tech A/V material as it is listed in many scattered sources.

Computer-based Data Banks

As previous sections have mentioned, data bases available both on-line and off-line have been appearing over the last eight to ten years, sponsored by societies, not-for-profit organizations, government agencies, and commercial firms. At first, such tape services (all on magnetic tape) could only be distributed via leases to an individual, company, or group, for exclusive use of the lessee. Then a period of greater flexibility came along, with organizations gaining the right to offer services to others, paying fees for such service to the tape owners.

Now we are in an era when the average university should weigh carefully the costs of obtaining and operating its own data base tapes. There are many hidden costs, and delays in starting service are common because of the work needed to match specifications of the tape to the computers and programs at hand.

In view of the availability of on-line service at several not-for-profit sources, as well as at least two commercial firms, many universities permit their librarians to act simply as middlemen, providing campus personnel with information about service bureaus offering on-line and off-line searches, both current and retrospective.

The medical profession has an advantage over other fields in that the National Library of Medicine has a service known as MEDLINE. This service gives health science libraries access to back files of data appearing in *Index Medicus,* as well as related data, at a nominal fee since it is a government agency. In other fields one must go to service bureaus for the most part.

A few of the major data banks available in machine-readable form are listed below. The field is changing quickly, so compilations soon get out of date. However, one publication which gives a description of many data bases is the following:

Schneider, John H. and others. *Survey of Commercially Available Computer-Readable Bibliographic Data Bases.* Washington, D.C.: American Society for Information Science, 1973. 197 p.

Major features of over seventy-five data bases are described. Includes both U.S. and foreign commercial firms. Primarily related to science and engineering. Based on November 1972 data.

Another listing of data bases may be found in the *Encyclopedia of Information Systems and Services.*

Data Bases

Listed below are some of the science and engineering data bases available on magnetic tape for computer searching. The beginning date for the information coverage is indicated.

BA-Previews—Based on *Biological Abstracts* and *BioResearch Index.* 1969-   .

CA-Condensates—Based on *Chemical Abstracts.* July 1968-   .

CAIN—Based on *Bibliography of Agriculture.* 1969-   .

COMPENDEX—Based on *Engineering Index.* 1969-   .

ERIC—Based on *Research in Education.* 1966-   .

GEO-REF—Based on data from about two thousand serials in geology. 1967-   .

INSPEC—Based on *Physics Abstracts, Electrical and Electronics Abstracts,* and *Computer and Control Abstracts.* 1969-   .

MEDLINE—Based on MEDLARS, covering the biomedical literature. 1970-   .

NUCLEAR SCIENCE ABSTRACTS—Based on this abstracting service. June 1966-   .

PSYCHOLOGICAL ABSTRACTS—Based on this abstracting service. 1967-   .

SCISEARCH—Based on the life sciences journals covered in *Current Contents* and *Science Citation Index.* April 1972-   .

SPIN—Based on data from over sixty journals in physics and astronomy. July 1970-   .

USGRDR—Based on the *U.S. Government Research & Development Reports* (and its successors). 1970-   .

Notes

[1]Mary L. Good, "Primary Publications: Problems, Progress," *Chemical & Engineering News* 52, no. 34 (August 26, 1974): 30-31.

[2]"Record of the Conference on the Future of Scientific and Technical Journals," *IEEE Transactions on Professional Communication* PC-16, no. 3 (September 1973).

Index

Index

211